Soccer's Dynamic Shortsided Games

First Edition

Soccer's Dynamic Shortsided Games

by

Andrew Caruso

Edited by

Richard Diedrichsen

Dedication

This book is the result of a lifetime of mentoring from clinicians, licensing staff, youth coaches, and countless soccer personalities who have allowed me a glimpse of the great game of soccer. Just as I have learned from veterans and World Cup champion players and coaches, I have also learned as much from enthusiastic beginning young players and coaches.

I thank them all and dedicate this work to them.

Library of Congress Catalog Card Number: 96-92006

ISBN: 0-9651020-0-9

Contents

Dedication i

Introduction v

Developing Players Through Dynamic Shortsided Games

Part I

Coaches' Favorites - The Most Effective Shortsided Games

1. Bruce Arena's Attack (6 v 6 + 4 N) 3
2. Pat Farmer's Fun (5 v 5 + 4N) 5
3. Jim Lennox's Lanes (3 + 2N v 3 + 2N + K) 9
4. Tony Waiters' Training Tournament (3 v 3) 11
5. Jeff Tipping's Transition (3 v 3, Functioning as 2 v 1) 13
6. Leslie Gallamore - Heading Layoff and Penetration 17
7. Chris Sweeney's Volley - (2 v 2 through 6 v 6) 19
8. Charlie Duccilli's Warm-up - Keep Away with Direction 21
9. Chris Malone & Colin Lindores' Change in Point of Attack . . . 25
10. Wiel Coerver's Many Goals 29
11. Ron Viewager's Heading Games 33
12. Jape Shattuck's Special Situations To Goal 35
13. Anson Dorrance's Direct Attack 37
14. Ron Quinn's Attack 39
15. Alan Wade's Midfield Probing 43
16. Gary Palmisano's Inside-Out/Outside-In 49
17. Quakertown's Team Shape for Youth 53
18. Jim Tonrey's First Touch 59
19. John Elliff's Target Penetration 63
20. Sarah Ferland and Meghan Cepetelli's Finishing School 67
21. Bobby Clark's Cover - The Essence of Defense 73
22. Barry Gorman's Shootout 79
23. Center Lane Neutrals - Chris Petricelli 83
24. Penn State Half Field Scrimmage 87

Part II: Basic Questions and Concepts of Coaching

25. How to Run Tryouts and Choose the Team 91
26. How to Evaluate Players for Positions 93
27. How to Design Training for Specific Ages 95
28. How to Recognize and Design Quality Exercise 97
29. How to Use Keep Away 99
30. Why Choose Soccer As a Sport, Or What Makes It Fun? . . . 101
31. How to Maintain Safety Around the Goal 103
32. How Tony Dicicco, Joe Machnik, Jeff Tipping & Greg Deutsch Train Goalkeepers for Excellence and Safety 107
33. How Ball Touches Relate to Player Development 117
34. How to Use 1 v 1 Formats 121
35. How to Observe a Match 125
36. Smallsided - Numbers for a Specific Purpose 128
37. Shortsided vs 11 Aside 132

Bibliography 134

This book is written as a reference book and for general content. Therefore, a one time quick reading, devoting a bit more time to Part II is appropriate.

Thereafter, reference back to a specific activity will ensure proper use of a given activity.

Hopefully this will offer variety, fun and additional ball touches to your training program. Most of all it should offer meaningful technical improvement because players are performing an abundance of technical skills in a tactical (shortsided game) environment.

Furthermore, blank space has been provided for your own wrinkles, variations, comments, etc.

Introduction

Developing Players through Dynamic Shortsided Games

This book is designed for experienced and enlightened coaches who realize the importance of dynamic shortsided games in training girls, boys, men, and women. It is the product of coaching young athletes at all levels, training soccer coaches at clinics and licensing courses, and sharing ideas with many of the top coaches in America and Europe.

The first part of this book contains suggestions for shortsided games designed for all ages; while most of these activities are more prevalent at the college and high school level, they can be used as they are or easily adapted for young players as well. A look at the contents will reveal the names of leading college and youth coaches who use these particular games and activities to develop many of the best soccer players in the nation. Obviously, the lions share of player development comes from within the player.

The second part contains answers to the most fundamental questions asked by youth and school coaches. This section deals with basic concepts and activities of coaching, from philosophy to practical tips for organizing and developing field players and goalkeepers in practice and games.

Also included is a long overdue section on safety, as well as goalkeeper training from the standpoint of safety. Proper keeper training improves both the performance and safety of the entire team. Coaches who believe that safe goalkeeping is simply a matter of technique should consider what the leading keeper trainers have to say in Chapter 32.

This book does not pretend to be the last word on any of these subjects, but rather a part of the continuing dialogue that fosters the growth of coaches, players, and the great game of soccer.

While no enlightened coach questions the value of shortsided training in developing players, less experienced coaches may confuse shortsided games with simple street or backyard soccer. Though both forms of the game are essential to success, they are very different. Street and backyard soccer adapt the rules to accommodate the limitations of the physical environment, while shortsided training adapts the rules to overcome the limitations of the players.

Coaches must continue to advocate street and backyard soccer, so that their players will gain the ball touches and decision making experience necessary for excellence. Backyard Soccer is "practice," and "practice makes permanent." Because it is more internal and self-directed, this brand of soccer is in most ways more productive than line drills, full field scrimmages, or exercises that eliminate defensive pressure.

Coaching is creating environments that teach or train. The most dynamic form of training is the shortsided game, adapted for a teaching purpose. This environment accelerates learning because it involves all four elements of the game: technique, tactics, fitness, and psychological. This is economic training at its best because it can focus on and develop any specific skill.

For example, these games develop fitness at the same time that they develop technical and tactical skills. Merely running laps or wind sprints develops aerobic fitness, but **these** games develop match related fitness. Young players will be reasonably fit if practices are competitive and rigorous. Furthermore, the pacing element, a major fitness tactic, can only be learned in a competitive game environment with the ball. Pacing means knowing when to sprint, jog, or walk. Since no one can sprint for ninety minutes, knowing when not to sprint is important.

Coaches who study their craft or take licensing courses are familiar with shortsided games as a regular component in their training sessions. They have learned to run through the progressions from fundamental to match related to match condition stages. The approach taken in this book does not question this progression; it merely reflects the thinking of the nation's top coaches as to how much time should be spent at each stage. Today, the emphasis should be on match condition activities, with at least 2/3 of the session devoted to these shortsided games, and at least 20 minutes devoted to unrestricted play.

These progressions and competitive games are based on ball contact, scoring goals, activity, and fun. They provide fitness training using the ball, and emphasize match skills; that is, the right combination of technique and tactic for the circumstance. Therefore, these games are superior to talk, line drills, and passive exercises. Talking does not improve control, dribbling, or scoring; it does little for decision making, and nothing for fitness!

The emphasis here is on attacking skills, since there is no meaningful defense until players have command of the ball. This is ideally achieved around the age of twelve. Before this age virtually all instruction is aimed at developing control and confidence with the ball. Dribbling is the pivotal skill at this stage, since dribbling skills (moves, control, lifts, shielding) are the basis of all player development.

To maximize the development of each player with these games, the coach should provide as much parity as possible. Occasional mis-match activities may not be avoidable, and a small amount may build confidence or challenge the mentally tough player; but parity usually balances the challenge with the chance of success. Well-matched teams, therefore, keep players in tune with the game. Children in street soccer find a myriad of methods of achieving parity. We should take their example and learn from it.

If these games serve as a starting point for your own adaptations, the book will be a success. Try your own "wrinkles" with your particular players in mind. The best coaches find ways to develop all of their players. In order to do this, a complete written plan is usually necessary until the coach is extremely experienced. A clear mental plan is **always** a necessity.

As a role model and leader, the coach often has much more influence than he or she may realize. Therefore, every practice for every player should be a positive experience. When players feel that the coach has confidence in them, they invariably gain confidence in themselves and play better. Positive individual attention, especially with the weakest players, pays off not only in player development but in human development.

This book will help you to exploit the shortsided approach to coaching to the fullest extent.

Part I

Coaches' Favorites
The Most Effective Shortsided Games

1 · Bruce Arena's Attack (6 V 6 + 4N)

Purpose

To develop penetration and goal line play in order to finish. Also to create an awareness of target players.

Exercise

Use approximately 44 yards by 60 yards to full size goals. Vary number of players from four to six a side. Two extra players along each goal line are free to move (along the goal line only) to support the attack at all times. They are only neutral in the sense that they are not marked by defenders, and they do not score themselves. Their function is to receive a pass, then lay it off for a teammate to shoot. At first no shot can be taken until one of these support players receives and passes the ball. Or score one point for a general goal, and three points for a goal resulting from support. Rotate players in and out of the exercise every five to eight minutes.

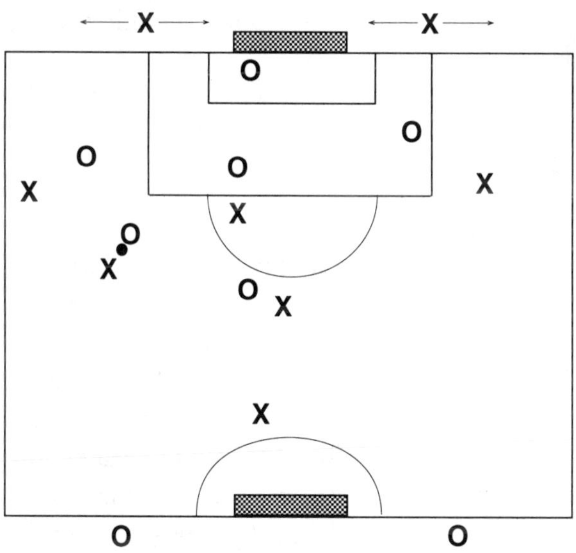

Diagram 1: Penetrating to goal line is a useful and desired behavior.

Discussion, Variations, Coaching Points

Demand constant support from the extra players. They will need to move quickly and constantly. Man-to-man marking is usually required in this activity; however, if training for defense, it is more important that players concentrate on "cover." Cover is a major weakness in the United States, due to the overemphasis on man-to-man marking. This game has countless variations, according to the intended purpose.

For example:

1. Focus on quick support by requiring two-touch soccer. This is effective with an advanced team age fifteen and up. One touch would really be a challenge for the most advanced players.
2. Focus on change of field and crossing by requiring passes from and to the opposite (weak) side of the field.
3. Focus on transition by demanding quick counter attack and quick defensive organization.
4. Focus on defensive technique through man-to-man defense.
5. Focus on defensive tactics through cover provided by second defenders.
6. Focus on long range shooting by eliminating or limiting goalkeepers.
7. Focus on fitness by using only one extra player on each goal line. This player can offer constant support on either the strong or weak side.
8. Focus on combination play for advanced levels by awarding five points for goals scored by a third man-on receiving the pass from the extra neutral player.

General Coaching Point

Coaching stoppages in shortsided play should be infrequent so as not to disrupt the unity and fun of play. Stop for important points only. Create a clear picture for your players by stopping them with a command to "freeze." Be brief and to the point, generally 10-45 seconds. Then restart by recreating the coaching point being made. Usually the first pass or two must be free. The sandwich approach is a positive and most successful method for correcting player mistakes. Start with a positive opening, make a clear correction, then offer a positive application of how this will help the player. For example, "Your run was well timed, Sarah; that is why you contacted the ball. But from six yards out, accuracy is needed. Use the inside of the foot. Show the surface. If you use the inside of your foot, you're going to score more goals."

2 · Pat Farmer's Fun (5 v 5 +4N)

Purpose

To promote possession, develop change in point of attack, and develop perimeter play use of the whole field.

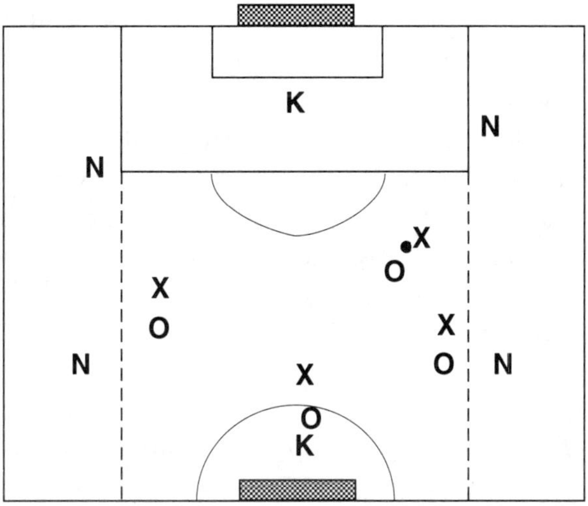

Diagram #2: Here 44 yards by 44 yards using 4 players on a team creates a 4 v 4 v 4 rotation, providing an ideal work/rest ratio of 2/1.

Exercise

For 6 v 6 or 8 v 8, use approximately half field, with full width; for smaller sides, use penalty area width. Use full size goals and keepers. Neutral players play for both teams, moving freely in their space, but not entering the field of play. They can be generally limited to one or two touches, and the ball must always be moving. Rotate neutral players as a team into the game every three to six minutes, or after every goal. Reward the winning team by keeping them on or letting them rest, according to the situation (temperature, fatigue, and fun are all factors). What players desire ultimately determines these rewards.

Discussion, Variations, Coaching Points

Interval training is good soccer coaching. This is an ideal rotation for a rigorous workout, since it provides one rest period to two work intervals.

Possession and connecting on 8 or more passes should be easy with 4 neutrals, so be sure to demand forward movement, going to goal and finishing. **Possible variations include:**

1. Focus on more movement from the neutrals by providing only one neutral on each side.
2. Focus on the overlap by allowing field players to interchange with neutrals whenever the field player overlaps the neutral.
3. Focus on penetration by restricting teams to 5 or fewer passes before shooting.
4. Focus on possession tactics by requiring that the team with the lead use the clock by trying to string together a certain number of passes. Score a point for 10 or more passes, a point for a goal, and 3 points for 10 passes plus a goal. This might force the defending team to play high pressure defense, challenging the attackers to play attractive attacking soccer.
5. Focus on the match related stage by placing a defender in the neutral area.
6. For younger groups, use a smaller area with 3 v 3 or even 2 v 2 plus a neutral player on each side. Rotations in this case are likely to take place every 2 or 3 minutes. Depending upon your purpose, score 3 points for goals off the dribble, or 3 points for goals off a combination.

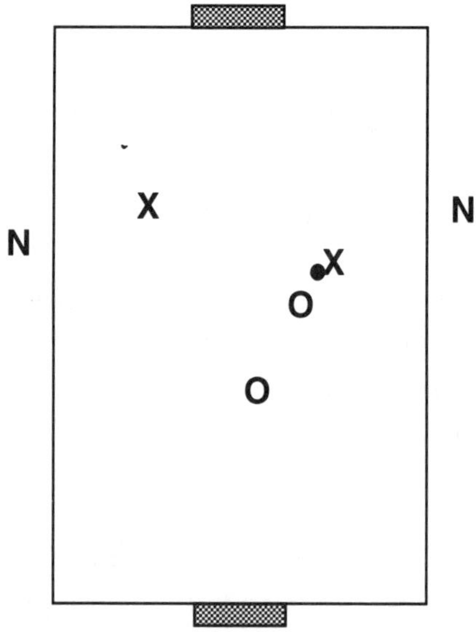

Diagram #3: Rotations in 2 v 2 are likely to take place every 2 or 3 minutes.

General Coaching Point

Teams from ages 5-14 work on possession virtually all the time, while high level teams work less on possession (but still the majority of the time). There are occasions where training emphasizes direct (rapid penetration) play, but no neutrals would be used in that instance. Even in direct play there is a desire for possession, but penetration, especially with the long ball, involves more risk. Much of the decision-making in the attack involves the choice between the safety of possession and the risk of penetration.

3 · Jim Lennox's Lanes (3 + 2N v 3 + 2N + Keepers)

PURPOSE

To develop crossing skills and finishing from the cross.

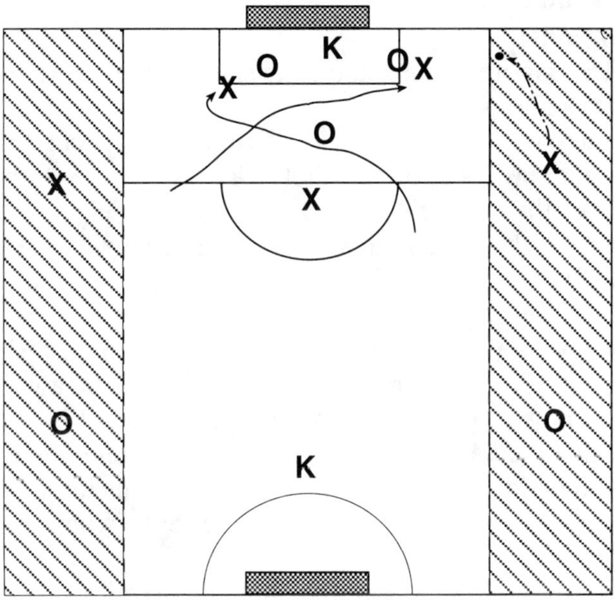

Diagram #4: Like the previous game, restricted ground with channel players fosters possession and crossing success.

EXERCISE

Use half of a full field and a full team, 10 or more players, with full size goals and goalkeepers. In the diagram, the game is 3 v 3, but sides of 4 or 5 would be equally constructive. Channel players are restricted to one touch for short passes, two touches for crossing. They look for field players who are filling the attacking slots.

DISCUSSION, VARIATIONS, COACHING POINTS

Filling slots near post, far post, and behind penalty spot should be done from wide angle runs. The first run should be from the back post across the goalmouth. Channel players must serve a specific type of pass to an attacker: ground ball pull backs to the penalty spot, driven balls to near post, and lofted balls to far post. This environment provides time and space for such mindful decisions. Mindless decisions (blind passes) do not develop mindful players. In order to upset the defense, the ball must move inside-out and outside-in. Merely coming straight down the flank will not provide problems to a defense. This is a great environment for defenders as well as attackers. Defenders will learn to get the ball outside, but should control the ball, not just clear it.

Possible variations:

1. With 16 or more players and an assistant, consider two separate stations.
2. Once the basic activity is productive, focus on decision-making and direct play by allowing shots directly on goal without sending the ball to the channel.
3. To focus on the match related stage, add a single defender to the channel, while the two channel players become members of both in order to serve the ball.
4. To improve communication between crosser and finisher, remove the neutral ground restriction. Crosses should be away from the keeper, and **slotted to beat the final defender**. Players should be taught that the ball must be sent through the opening that the nearest defenders (to the server) provide. This improves the connection between server and receiver even when there is pressure.
5. To focus on building out of the back, do not allow the keeper to send the ball to the channel.

General Coaching Point

Ideally, coach only one theme with only three or four aspects of the activity in a given session. It is not productive to focus on too many aspects of the game at once. It is best to have a thread of continuity for the entire practice, where all activities for the session are related to one skill. When this ideal practice is not always possible, try to relate several parts of the practice together. Progressions should start with the simple and move to the complex. Such a carefully developed sequence greatly enhances player development. Nearly every progression should incorporate shooting at goal with some form of pressure. A goal with a net fosters good shooting habits; when there is no net, players often develop the bad habit of shooting at the goalkeeper.

4 · Tony Waiters' Training Tournament (3 v 3)

Purpose

To provide abundant ball contact, to develop support, penetration, mental toughness, and fitness.

Exercise

Use a set of small fields, 20 yards by 30 yards, with small goals 1-2 yards wide, without goalkeepers. Restart all out of bounds with a throw-in. After every 6-10 minutes, take a one-minute break, then begin second round with winners playing winners, losers playing losers. The third round pits double winners against each other, splitters against each other, and double losers against each other. Continue until there is a single winner, but allow every team to keep playing games.

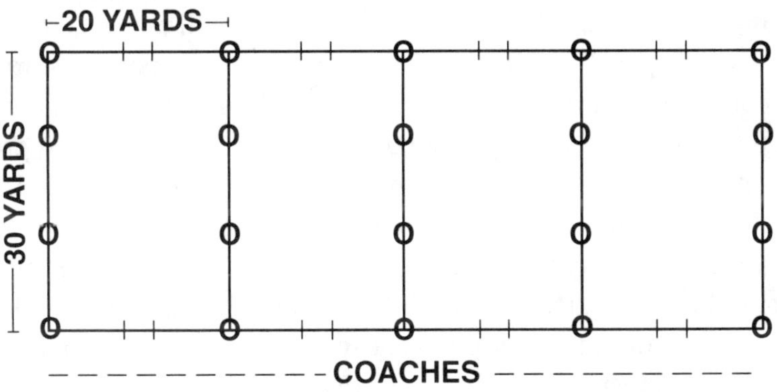

Diagram #5: Accu-goals approximately 2 yards wide would be excellent for this activity.

Discussion, Variations, Coaching Points

This is "micro soccer," a perfect activity, which simulates "street soccer" as nearly as humanly possible in this day and age. The coach moves from one group to another making very simple coaching points, especially in regard to combinations. Create as much team parity as possible, changing teams if necessary. But be patient enough to allow for a team to adjust its tactics; they may get right back in the game. This is a great practice when two teams are joined together. Encourage hard work, getting the ball into play immediately, and quick transitions. This, along with the highly competitive nature of the tournament, teaches mental toughness! The final game should be observed by the coach, and other teams, to give it some importance. For variety, run a round-robin or partial round-robin tournament, with a final game between the two teams with the best record. High level teams should use "accu-goals" (32″x 52″) so that all three finishing dimensions (long range accuracy, power shots, and skillful dribbling) are developed. Avoid endless talk. Stop a given group that may need help, or the entire group for a point relating to all groups. But avoid settling anything that players can and will settle by themselves in a few moments. To develop the concept of depth and width, use the same activity with 4 v 4. But teach the concept of depth and width before demanding it in competitive games.

General Coaching Point

Always enhance your activity with restrictions, scoring, and/or numbers that create numerous chances to repeat a skill with a good chance of success. When players have had numerous successful repetitions, relax the restriction. This will usually create more realistic decision making, where the players may use the particular skill less often, but at the proper time. Next remove the restriction entirely. Finally, devote the last 10-20 minutes to totally uninterrupted play, allowing players to demonstrate what they've learned. Meanwhile, the coach can refine his or her diagnosis of team and individual strengths and weaknesses. Players must have the opportunity to think for themselves, especially during this final part of the session. They must be allowed to make errors, innovate, create, and even fail without fear. Removing the fear of failure enhances both skill development and fun.

5 · Jeff Tipping's Transition (3 v 3 Functioning as 2 v 1)

PURPOSE

To develop transition, combinations that penetrate, to develop support, defense, and fitness. On any given day use this exercise for only one purpose with possibly 2 or 3 specific aspects.

EXERCISE

Use a playing area of 20 yards by 30 yards, with small goals. The player or goalie is not allowed to use his or her hands, and must remain on the goal line. Play 3 v 3 with a line dividing the halves of the field.

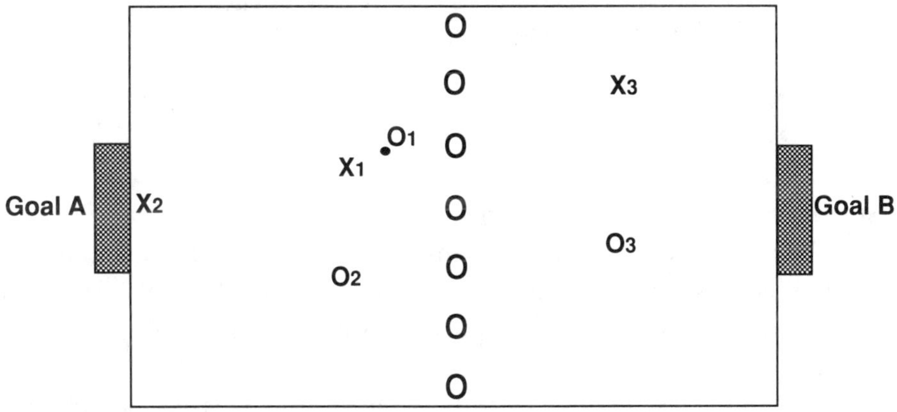

Diagram #6: O1 with ball and O2 are attacking goal; X3 and O3 wait until ball comes back to their side of the field. If X1 wins the ball or the O team scores, X1 and X2 begin to attack goal B. But only that player who passes the ball to X3 can cross the midline and help attack goal B. Thus, if X2 makes the pass, he and X3 attack, while X1 merely remains behind to defend on the next transition.

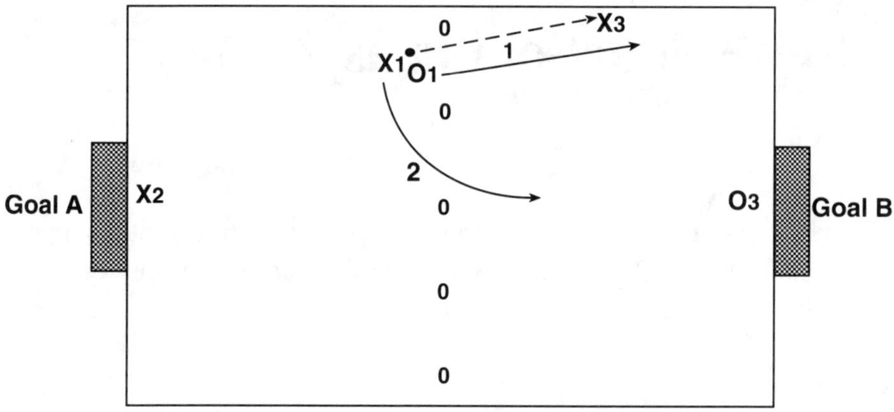

Diagram #7: O1 rapidly retreats to defend against X3. O1 is rapidly retreating to defend against X3. Players for team X try to combine (with a wall pass, layoff, or overlap) with X3. The X player who is not involved must remain behind. No one player is the keeper throughout; all roles are interchangeable. This is great for players learning to pace themselves and to help teammates who are temporarily winded.

Discussion, Variations, Coaching Points

This activity involves much thinking, and takes a while to understand. Nevertheless, it is well worth the time and effort. Attacking players learn to support and not hide. The final player learns the functional skills of a sweeper, namely cover and communication.

Demand quick counterattacks from the team in possession, which will force excellent recovery from the defenders.

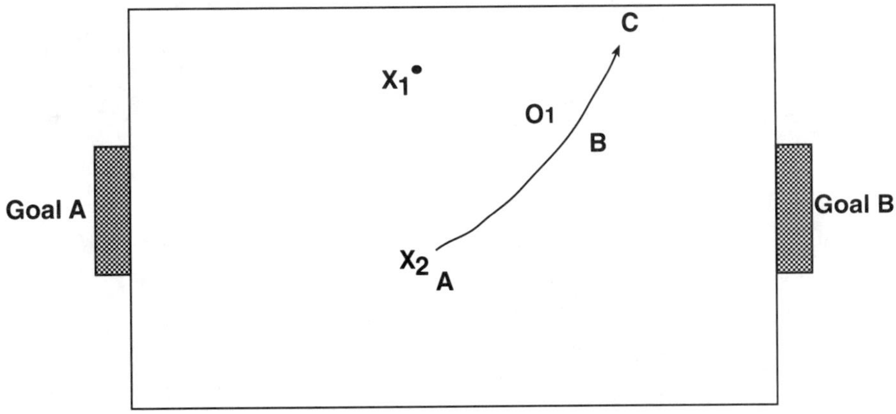

Diagram #8: Position A and C are good choices, because X1 can make a pass to X2. Position B is not helpful; player X2 must get to location C with a hard accelerated run.

General Coaching Point

If an activity is worth doing only once, it is probably not worth doing at all. It may take a few minutes to learn a new activity, but the real value comes only after the activity is understood, and decision making becomes a part of it. Therefore, it is better use of time to do about 10-20 exercises regularly than to introduce something totally new every session. However, each time you prescribe a familiar exercise, add a different "wrinkle" or coaching point. The best wrinkles are those tailored to a specific player or team. In this manner, the coach teaches soccer, not activities.

6 · Leslie Gallimore's Volley Heading Layoff & Penetration

PURPOSE

To develop heading skills, as well as support, one touch, and penetration using the head and foot.

EXERCISE

This is like volleyball, but with a twist that ensures full participation by everyone: the target player, O1 or X1 in the diagram, must play the ball back to a teammate before it can be sent to the opponent's side. In other words, the target player can only set the ball for a teammate, and cannot play it to the opponent. Generally, one bounce is permitted.

At lower levels it is tennis (allowing one bounce), but as players develop and gain experience or are high level, it is played as volleyball (no bounce).

Use a playing area of 8 yards by 30 yards. Each team of 5 players is allowed only 6 touches before the ball must be played to the opponent. No player may touch the ball three times consecutively. Play begins with an underhand ball thrown to your own target player (O1 or X1 in the diagram), who returns it to his or her own team. That receiver can then send the ball to the opposite's side.

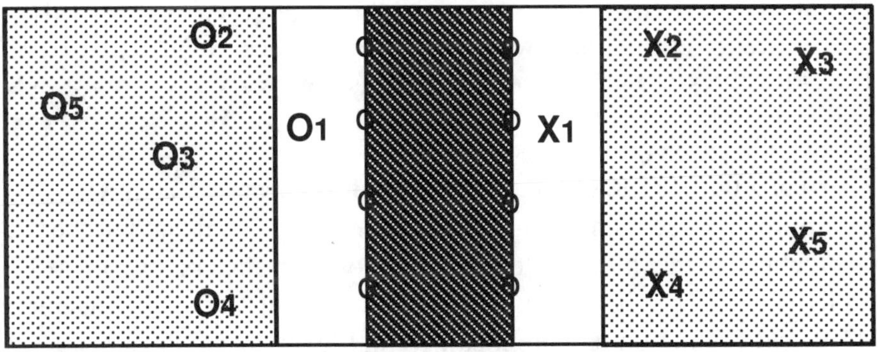

Diagram #9: Over the Net Soccer Volley; play begins with an underhand ball thrown to your own target player (O1 or X1), who returns it to his/her own team before it can be sent to opposite team.

Service is to the shaded area. Play to a predetermined score (11 is common) or for a predetermined amount of time. Score as in volleyball, where the serving team can win a point, the receiving team can only win the serve. Rotate as in volleyball, so that each player becomes the target.

Discussion, Variations, Coaching Points

This is excellent for developing heading skills, maintaining possession, and deciding when to penetrate. **Variations are many:**

1. To encourage heading, require at least one header per volley.
2. To further encourage heading with older players, count all marginal (in terms of in or out-of-bounds) air balls as in-bounds.
3. To develop control with younger players, require two touch play.
4. For chipping development, require service by foot; a simple lift to a teammate or a full chip to the opponent begins the volley.
5. Another service option is a correct throw-in, short to a teammate, or long to the opponent.
6. For younger players, allow two bounces.
7. For advanced players, require two touches, but one must be a header, except the service to the opponent
8. To increase the difficulty for advanced players, add a defender to each side. At first, the defender may have to be limited in terms of mobility or contact; for example, the defender can only head the ball.
9. For development of sending and receiving long balls, increase the playing area.
10. For development of tight control, decrease the area.
11. To increase the pace of the game, alternate every service, and score for each volley, whether serving or receiving.
12. Play the same game with numbers as low as 2 v 2.

General Coaching Point

Every practice should include a heading drill because it is unwise to run an entire practice on heading. If the heading can be related to the day's practice, so much the better. For the younger players, use a "friendly" ball for heading activities; the lightweight 10 ounce Finisher or the #4 World Champion ball are ideal. With the youngest players, a volleyball can be used.

7 · Chris Sweeney's Volley (2 v 2 through 6 v 6)

Purpose

To develop ball control with all body parts, quick reactions, and flexibility; to open the abdominal area; to improve communication and support.

Exercise

This is just like volleyball, using soccer skills. The game can be played on a tennis, handball, or squash court, or over flat-faced goals, with or without the net.

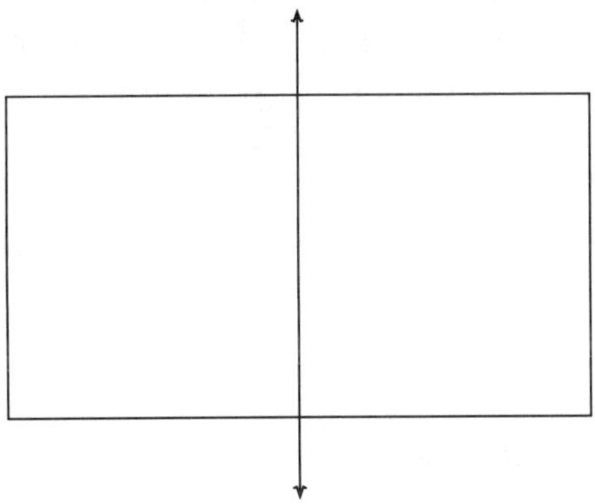

Diagram #10: Over the Net is a great camp, tournament, or rainy day activity. A Wiel Coerver goal can be used as the net.

Discussion, Variations, Coaching Points

This is a great camp, tournament, picnic, or training activity that can be used as a cool-down after more rigorous activities, in intense heat, or small spaces. As a warm-up, it gets players involved immediately. Start with the first two players and add others as they arrive.

Remember to use a lightweight ball. A volleyball can be used to introduce younger players to this game.

Encourage the use of the correct body part for the situation. As competence is gained, encourage good tactics such as very specific pace and placement of returns.

For younger players, allow a bounce as in tennis. Restrict advanced players to use of the inside (or outside) of foot. Advanced players could also be required to set each other up as opposed to merely returning the ball. Another variation that is sure to challenge the best of players is to add a second ball. This will increase the tactical and technical challenge, and especially the fun!

Further variations can be found in the previous game in Chapter 6.

General Coaching Point

Coaching today's athletes demands an understanding of the psychological element of sports, even at younger ages. The old approaches that stirred soldiers to battle, the intense pep talks, threats, and cheers do not prepare young players for games of skill and decision making.

Clear, simple, scientific techniques such as relaxation, concentration, and visualization have proven their worth in athletic psychological growth. Such basics as realistic goal setting can make a positive difference in development. John Wooden attributed much of his success in coaching basketball to his constant focus on practice skills used in the game. **He knew that winning was simply a by-product of executing these practice skills well**. In his 40 years of coaching, John Wooden never even mentioned winning!

8 · Charlie Ducilli's Warm-up Keep Away with Direction

PURPOSE

A game-related passing/receiving warm-up.

EXERCISE

Use the area from the 18 yard line to midfield for 7 v 7 or 8 v 8. The touchlines of the full field become the goals. Generally, there are no keepers. Goals are scored by dribbling over either touchline. However, there is no stoppage after scoring a goal or winning possession, a team immediately attacks the other touchline. Therefore, the game has direction, but the direction is always changing.

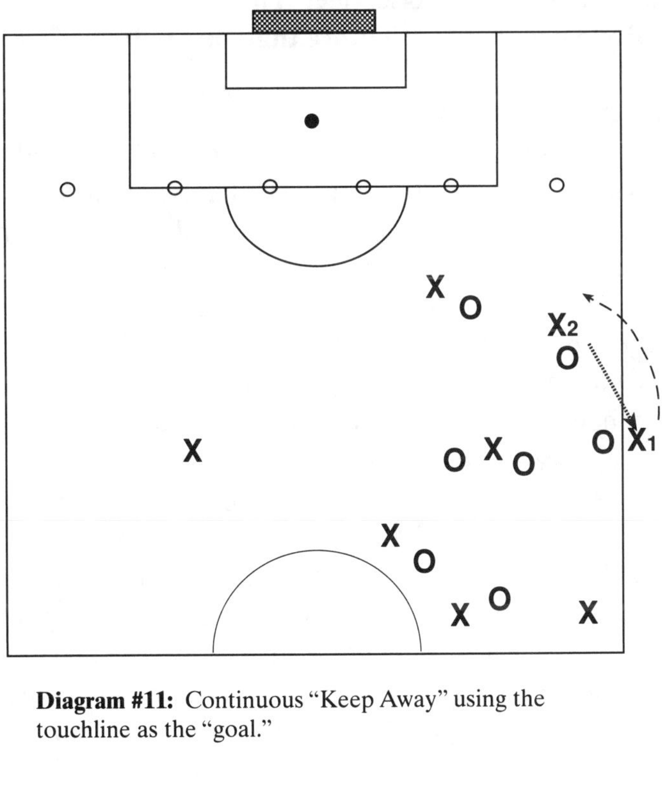

Diagram #11: Continuous "Keep Away" using the touchline as the "goal."

Discussion, Variations, Coaching Points

The teams can be made up to a specific purpose that is related to the session's plan. For example, putting all the defenders on one team may improve communication, while putting all attackers on the other team may improve connection. Also, teams do not always have to be equal in number; unequal numbers are sometimes better.

To develop the role of the "schemer," allow that player to be neutral, always playing for the attacking side. To find out who is best suited for that role, allow each player some time to be the neutral player.

Keepers normally work with free kick specialists in the opposite goal of the full field during this activity. But adding keepers to this game adds a new dimension; they will be diving at the feet of dribblers attempting to score. Obviously, this requires keepers who have been fully trained in this skill (for suggestions on diving, see Chapter 22 Goalkeeper Safety).

Keepers in this game will also get a great deal of practice with distribution, a weakness in soccer worldwide. **This is a great game day warm-up, especially when done with more than one ball.**

General Coaching Point

Warm-up activities should get both the body and the mind working; this requires a great deal of ball touches and decision making. Therefore, keep away in its many forms can be very helpful. A great training session begins with a great warm-up, one that is related to the topic for the day. Thus, if passing and receiving is the session's topic, a great deal of passing and receiving must take place during the warm-up.

Very few young players have the knowledge and discipline to properly warm up on their own. The most common mistake made by unsupervised players is a poor warm-up. These players usually begin by carrying a ball to the penalty area and taking direct kicks on goal before the muscles are warmed and stretched. This habit not only fails to prepare the players physically and mentally, it also sets them up for injury!

Therefore, the coach needs to ensure that each player has a proper warm-up. Proper warm-up has both a physical and mental component. The physical component increases the heart rate and breathing gradually, and generally produces a sweat. It involves numerous ball touches, starting with light dribbling, juggling, and short passing, with **intermittent stretching** after he muscles are warmed. Do not stretch cold muscles.

The mental component sharpens the players' awareness and prepares them for decision making. This stage of the warm-up is a good time for mental preparation such as visualization. Then players should progress to longer passing, heading, shooting, and match-related games like 3 v 1, 4 v 2, and 5 v 2, which require more energy and decision making. Shortsided games are a great warm-up component, especially when they include lots of movement, passing and receiving, and shooting on goal.

9 · Chris Malone & Colin Lindores' Change in Point of Attack

Purpose

To develop effective movement in changing the point of attack, especially in the finishing third of the field.

Exercise

Stage I of this game is play 3 v 3 and score by passing to one of the two corner goal players. The corner goal player immediately passes to the other corner goal player (simulates a change in point of attack) and immediately puts the ball back in play to the team who gave the ball (scored). Essentially the winners restart the game, instead of scoring and giving the ball to the opponent.

Stage II use approximately half the field, with a grid adjacent to the penalty area, as in the diagram. Teams can vary from 2 v 2 up to 5 v 5, but there are always 4 corner players.

Defenders may not intercept passes to corner players. When the attacking team strings five consecutive passes together, the defensive team must run and stand on the goal line, defending without the use of their hands. At this point the neutrals get involved.

Neutral target players (T1, T2, T3, T4) pass in the following pattern:

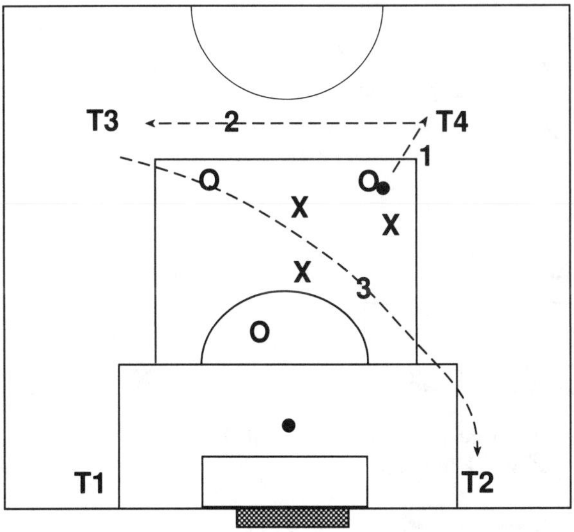

Diagram #12: Here the ball is first sent to a player positioned at midfield.

Note changes in the point of attack in midfield and the goal area. While neutral players pass the ball, attacking players time their runs to fill the slots properly to create a good shot at goal.

If, after five passes, the ball is passed directly to the goal line (as in Diagram #12), T1 must pass to T3 to allow time for the attackers to fill their slots. Obviously, by the time service 4 takes place, the X players in the grid should be on the goal line and the O players should be filling the slots and getting a shot on goal.

Keep score; alternate one grid team with the neutrals after about 10 minutes or when goals are scored. If scoring team feels rewarded by becoming neutrals, then rotate in this fashion. If they feel rewarded by continuing to play, allow them to continue playing. If the ball goes from the grid to a high player (as in Diagram #13), the change in point of attack takes place at midfield, so then the diagonal ball should be sent to the goal line before the service into the goal area.

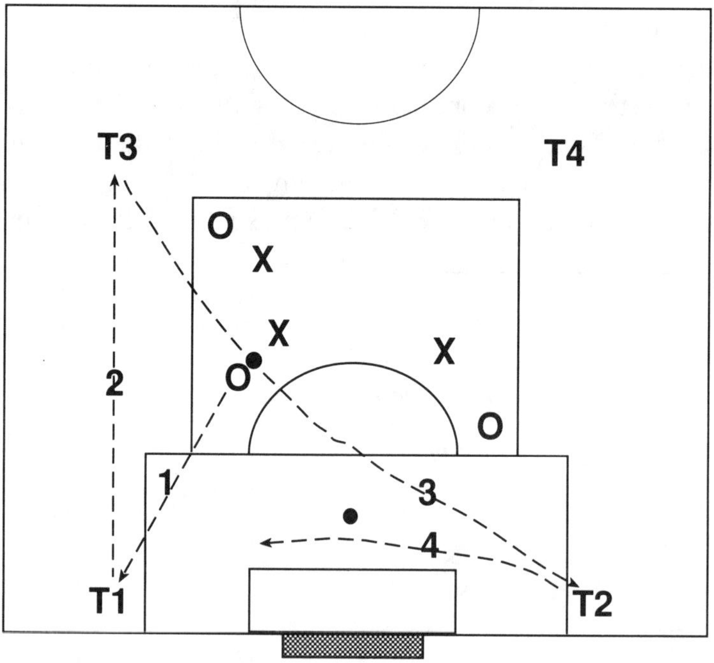

Diagram #13: Here the ball is first sent to a goal line player. Note the change in point of attack in goal area.

Discussion, Variations, Coaching Points

This game provides a great environment for developing transition, as well as excellent functional training for finishing skills. Get more players involved by increasing the size of the grid, or add a neutral player to the grid, who always plays for the attacking team.

Later on, a keeper can be added. Defenders can continue to play defense or simply become passive. This can also become a shortsided game with two full size goals, with or without keepers. Require that a change in point of attack be made before a shot can be taken.

For further development, require that a shot be taken after only one change in point of attack. For the most advanced groups, encourage or require alternating attack systems: first direct, then indirect. For further variety, emphasize a different kind of finish: head, volley, half volley, ground, etc., on each successive occasion that this exercise is used.

One or two resting or extra players can keep extra balls available for this activity.

One major coaching point in this game is the timing and direction of attacking runs. A run made too early is wasted; so is a run that is too direct, which makes the angle for receiving and shooting much more difficult. To fill the slots properly, teach your players to attack the near post by going across the goal at speed, attack the far post at a wide angle, and the area behind the penalty spot with an eye for the deflection or rebounding shot. Variations include scoring a point for five consecutive passes. Or, balls passed to neutrals can be air balls, which defenders can challenge for, instead of the usual free pass.

General Coaching Point

Always finish a training session with unrestricted, uncoached soccer with enjoyment as the focus of play. If you have done your job, you have taught the players plenty for one session. Now evaluate their learning as demonstrated in the shortsided game. Now reward your players by stepping back and letting them simply enjoy the game without further instruction or interruption.

10 · Wiel Coerver's Many Goals

Purpose

To develop all aspects of attacking, especially finishing, as well as transition and defending.

Exercise

Use half the field for the playing area, with goals set up on each line as in the diagram. The number of players per team can vary from 5 to 8. Either team can score on any of the 4 goals.

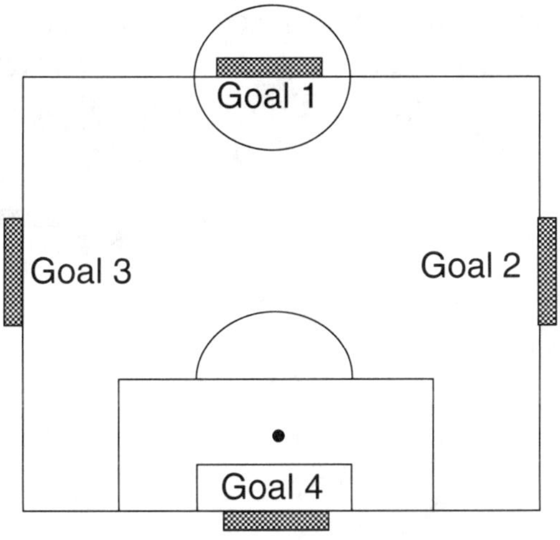

Diagram #14: Change in point of attack with long balls is often very effective.

Discussion, Variations, Coaching Points

Obviously, this game creates a great deal of shooting opportunities. But it provides even more opportunities to make quick transitions from attack to defense and also from defense to attack. Thus it is an excellent vehicle for teaching team shape on attack and defense.

This game encourages diagonal play, target play and decision making; when a goal area is over-crowded with defenders, attackers will learn to pull out and re-develop the attack elsewhere.

The game is also very good for developing man-to-man marking, and the vital skill of learning to look and play 360 degrees. Players that are unidirectional will quickly learn to view more of the field for attacking chances and defensive runs.

A good variation of this game is to limit players to 2 touches. This will force them to look around and anticipate even more.

Another variation, perhaps for younger players, would be to limit each team to scoring on two adjoining goals. Thus in the above diagram, team 'A' would shoot on goals 1 and 2, team B on goals 3 and 4.

Numerous other variations deal with the arrangement of the multiple goals. The goals can be placed on the field, allowing players to shoot from both sides of the goal, especially when using the flat faced goals.

Another variation is to place two goals on each end line, as in the diagram below. This encourages change in point of attack, man marking, and quick transition, and may be more manageable for younger players. This game can become directional, and can keep four goalkeepers involved, especially if a second ball is used. Or it can develop keeper footwork by requiring a single keeper to defend two goals.

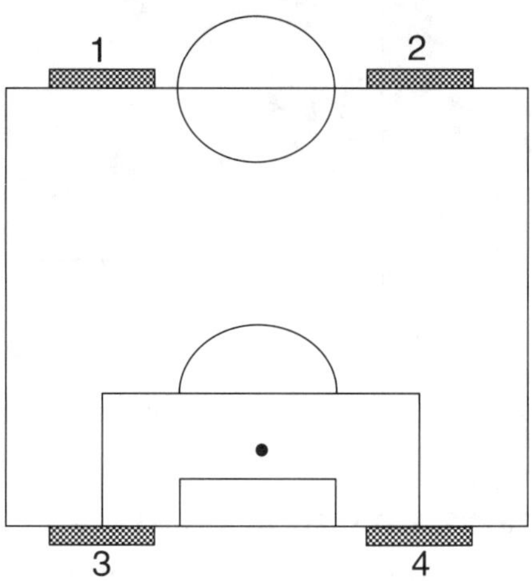

Diagram #15: This version of multiple goals relates strongly to change in point of attack in the goal area. All the above games are useful because they introduce variety while remaining competitive and match related. With full size goals and keepers, the game is basically real soccer with increased finishing possibilities. Another variation to create functional training is 4 v 4 with two neutral strikers always on the attacking team. This can be done with team 'A' attacking goals 1 and 3, team 'B' attacking goals 2 and 4 (refer to Diagram #14). To increase ball contact, play two groups of 4 v 4 rather than one group of 8 v 8. This would require two sets of traditional goals and two Wiel Coerver goals, which could be set-up as in the following diagram.

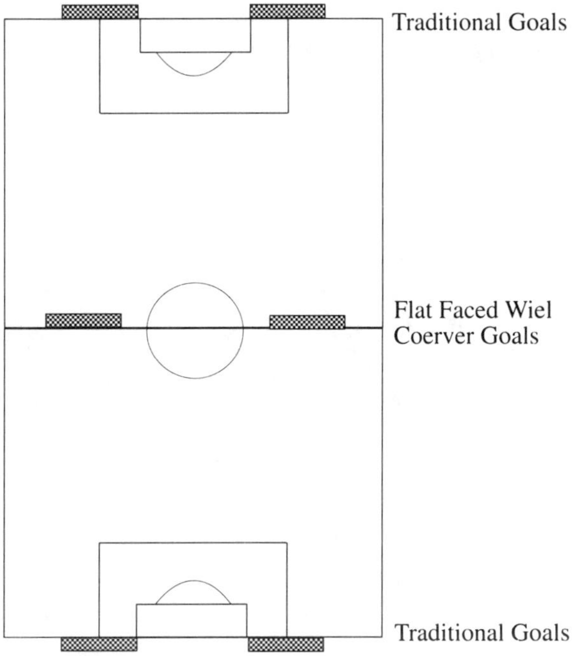

Diagram #16: This environment can easily serve 20-32 players (even more with rotating groups). Another method of making these multiple goal games exciting is to play 4 v 4 v 4 without stoppage. The team that scores immediately becomes the goalkeepers for the next game, while the resting team takes the field as quickly as possible. This game usually requires two passes before shooting, in order to give the new keepers time to get to their positions. However, playing without the two pass requirement forces defenders to immediately delay the attack, a very valuable skill. A second ball simply adds to the fun.

General Coaching Point

Fun is development! Without fun, players will not practice the skills they learn in training sessions, and will lack the enthusiasm which is the foundation of psychological strength. It is no coincidence that national team coaches from such soccer powers as Italy, England, Uruguay, and Scotland all make a major point of this when speaking to American coaches. Do they sense a problem that is difficult for us to see in ourselves?

11 · Ron Viewager's Heading Games

PURPOSE

Development of heading skills, quick transition, fitness, and communication.

EXERCISE

Use an area approximately 15 feet by 7 feet. The goals are the entire short ends. Play a 2 v 2 in this area. One player on the attacking team serves the ball (by hand) to his or her teammate for a header on goal.

The two defenders must stand on their goal line and defend without the use of hands. After a score, or as soon as the defenders win the ball, they attack the other goal in the same way, while the opponents rush back to defend against the header.

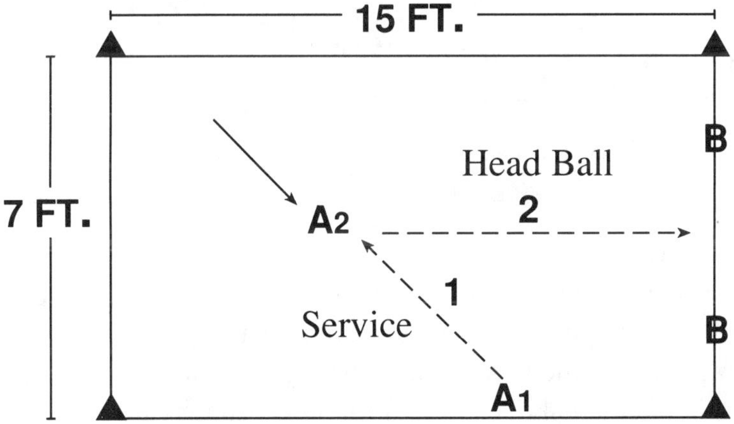

Diagram #17: In this exercise, players soon learn that quick transition helps a team to win. Adjust the grid area so that players can score, but only when they head the ball well. Play for 2-3 minutes or to a score of five goals. Leftover players retrieve balls to keep the exercise very active. Generally, a team is divided into 3 or 4 groups. Add excitment with diving headers or goals scored on the goal line. This is a great tournament activity.

DISCUSSION, VARIATIONS, COACHING POINTS

Quick transition helps a team to play good soccer and win. As players learn this, the pace, intensity, and fun increase.

Generally, the easiset place to score in this game is waist high, but when hands are used, the goal line becomes the best target area.

To involve more players, set up two or three groups, as in the diagram. Anson calls this 'bull pen.' Balls are served to the two competing players in the middle from both sides. The two competing players head it back to the server. Stage II has teams so that the X player always tries to get the ball to X, and the O player always to the O teammate. This obviously involves flick-ons **and** power headers.

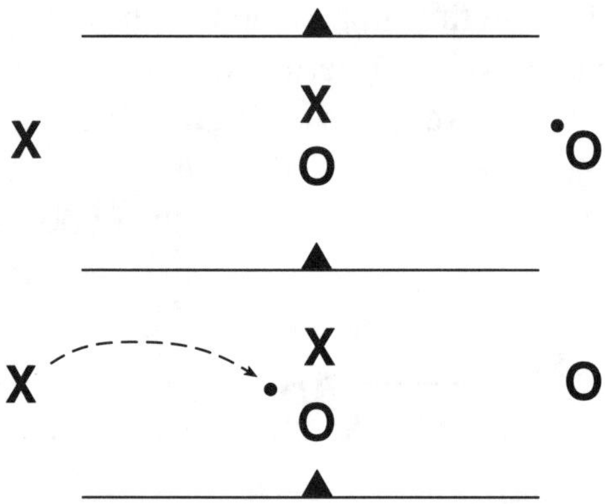

Diagram #18: 'Bull pen' is both fun and competitive.

General Coaching Point

While practice is important, youth coaches, no matter how dedicated, have other responsibilities that may prevent them from attending their team's practice. Yet their teams need the workout, in order to improve or at least maintain their skills and conditioning. Something as simple as a lack of fitness can cause danger to the players' safety. Whenever possible, the coach should arrange for an assistant or qualified parent volunteer to run the practice in his or her absence.

Fortunately, these shortsided games provide an excellent practice even when the head coach cannot attend. With a novice assistant coach, or volunteer parent, the activity itself becomes the teacher.

12 · Jape Shattuck's Special Situations To Goal

Purpose

To develop special situation plays that are trained for in match conditions and therefore work successfully in games.

Exercise

Using half a field or more with full size goals and keepers, divide all field players into two teams. While they play, the coach referees, calling all foolish (unnecessary) fouls that actually occur, especially in the penalty area.

Every two minutes, call an imaginary foul, and award a special situation alternately to each team. Award both teams the same number of opportunities, excluding the fouls that they actually commit. Keep score, keep it moving and competitive.

Each time you play this game, choose either cluster (below) as the emphasis, but work only on attack for the first session, and only on defense for the next session. Cluster I: Direct Free Kicks, Corner Kicks, Penalty Kicks. Cluster II: Indirect Free Kicks, Goal Kicks, Drop Kicks.

Discussion, Variations, Coaching Points

Use this game only after the team has learned the various set plays, otherwise, this session moves too slowly.

Some coaches do center kick-offs separately and early in the year because they use this play to set a style, psychology and team philosophy. It is never too early for this situation.

Throw-ins should be a part of nearly all shortsided games, and therefore are not in this session; however, if you need practice in this area, it can be easily incorporated. If throw-ins are not a problem, this game can substitute special situations for the throw-in; that is, when the ball goes out-of-bounds, it can be put back into play with a free kick. To speed up the pace, award the free kick to the team that retrieves the out-of-bounds ball, regardless of who knocked it out.

Coaching of special situations during scrimmage is preferable to isolated practice of these plays; it has much more carry over to matches. When players have fun practicing special situations, they will become better at it. Since a good portion of goals are scored from these situations, it is time well spent.

The question of whether to take free kicks quickly or slowly usually comes up in this game. Since each situation is some what different, no one approach is always right. Besides, it is often better to be unpredictable when taking free kicks, unless of course the team has very quick players or a free kick ace.

Certainly near the penalty area, quality execution of the free kick on goal is usually the important factor, so the pace would be slow and deliberate. Further from the scoring territory, time becomes more of a factor, especially if defenders are unprepared, or the keeper is off the line. Other factors that would play a role in quick or deliberate movement would be the team features such as fitness, health, aggression, or team depth. A final factor relates to the player taking the kick; what is his or her preference and strength?

Unlike most shortsided games, this game alone cannot replace small group rehearsal and practice for penalty kickers, corner kickers, free kicks and goal kicks. For specific special situations see Malcolm J. Simon and John Reeves "Soccer Restart Plays."

General Coaching Point

Great players are not made by talk, but by activity. Of two equally gifted players, which one would you want on your team - - the player who touched the ball 1,000,000 times and heard 10,000 words about soccer, or the player who touched the ball 10,000 times and heard 1,000,000 words about soccer?

Even if the speaker were Beckenbauer, the choice is clear. Once we realize that we might not quite be the Kaiser, even greater humility and understanding occurs. The game and ball have produced the great players; none were produced just by a coach. No great player will ever be produced without the ball and the game. Therefore, it seems to me, that anything that denies the ball and the game can be dangerous.

13 · Anson Dorrance's Direct Attack

Purpose

To develop direct play, especially by getting forward in a tight area; also to develop accurate service through lifts and throw-ins; and effective 1-2 moves, especially the layoff, in tight areas.

Exercise

This game is often played in the corner of the field from touchline to the side of the penalty area, but any area 40 yards by 20 yards will do. Use full size goals with keepers. Play 3 v 3, 4 v 4, or 5 v 5. The game is merely a shortsided game with no special restrictions; the size and shape of the playing area promotes the desired behaviors.

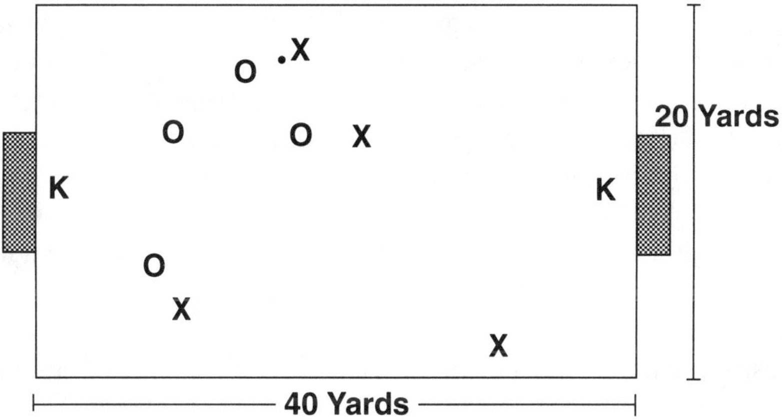

Diagram #19: The area shown is approximately 20 x 40 yards with full size goals. This is often done in the corner of the field from touchline to the side marks of the penalty area.

Discussion, Variations, Coaching Points

This game provides an excellent diagnostic/prescriptive coaching environment. But this level of coaching is recommended only to coaches who are highly prepared, fully experienced, or professional (full-time coach, highly licensed, played at high levels, etc.) Less experienced youth coaches (those below a C license level or who never played, for example)

example) should allow the ball and the activity to do most of the instruction. Since the game is played in match condition to full size goals, the transfer to games is easy and complete.

The game is economical because it involves a great deal of fitness. To maintain a high level of play, allow a 20-40 second rest every three or four minutes.

It can also be played as 4 v 4 v 4; rotate teams after a goal or every three minutes.

There are numerous restrictions that can force the use of various skills. For example, require a 1-2 move before a shot can be taken, or count two points for goals scored off the 1-2 move. The same could be done for layoffs or lifts. The narrow long grid forces direct long ball set-up by use of combinations.

General Coaching Point

Highly successful, highly professional coaches like Anson Dorrance are not afraid to devote all their energy to instruct a single player on one concept for a given shortsided game. It is not unusual at this level to devote a whole shortsided game of 40 minutes to working almost exclusively with one player. Such focus on one skill or concept of that session's topic can greatly improve a player.

Therefore, it makes very good sense to hold practice even with a few players. While some coaches would cancel, the enlightened coach uses the opportunity to coach one or two players for a single specific behavior. For these occasions, keep a record in your practice planner of one such idea for each player.

Of course, goalkeepers normally get special attention at regular practice sessions. While this is vital, coaches who treat their goalkeepers as if they are far more important than field players create a gap between their keepers and the rest of the team. Integrating keeper training with field players helps to unify and improve a team, but anything that over emphasizes these differences does not help the team or the game. Hotdogging and ostentatious uniforms do not belong on the field or in goal.

Never coach beyond your knowledge, leave room so that your suggestions (coaching points) are certain to be valid. Players are very astute in picking up on the coaches knowledge.

14 · Ron Quinn's Attack

Purpose

To penetrate to a target player, while maintaining a good chance of controlling the ball.

Exercise

This exercise will ultimately use the whole field, but begins using only the attacking third. While the rest of the team is doing some other activity at the other end of the field, train the two strikers on working together to receive passes in scoring range for a shot. Then add two central midfielders, training them to serve to the strikers. Next bring in the entire midfield, and soon after, add the wing midfielders. Teach players the basic options (Diagram #1 and #2) from both right and left sides. Then teach options #3 and #4, using several different players to overlap. Additional options may depend upon your team and individual player strengths. The others can learn this attack by participating in the upcoming scrimmage. For now, it is more effective that the others do not have the advantage of knowing these patterns. This part of the training session should be done in about 20 minutes to allow for a shortsided game of 60 minutes. This is the time required to effectively practice this attacking style. Naturally it must be practiced more than once.

Bring in the rest of the team to defend against the attackers. Require the trained team to use the target player in order to score. Once the trained team can execute this, add further restrictions: for example, no shot can be taken without a layoff or overlap.

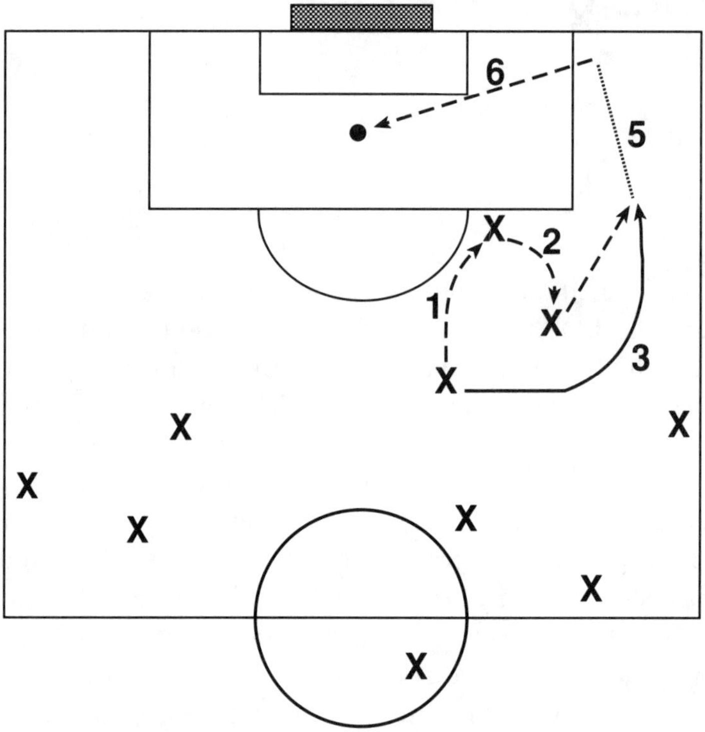

Diagram #20: All attacks are inside-out and then inside again; this creates confusion for the defense. Options: 1. Ball to "high" target player, served by anyone. 2. Layoff to low striker or even a midfielder. 3. Overlap by any player on weak or strong side. 4. Service to overlap. 5. Dribble to goal line (or early service, or layoff to another server). 6. Service near post, far post, or just beyond penalty spot.

Discussion, Variations, Coaching Points

A systematic attack allows for more improvisation and creativity because the entire team has a notion of a basic pattern with several options.

It is essential to get a great deal of repetition in match conditions of this activity, so the attack should regularly achieve a shot on goal. At first, defenders may have to begin by playing numbers down. For higher levels, get to match condition soon.

Teach the players' who receive the layoff from the target player to create time for the overlap; time can be created by dribbling, shielding, or by turning away from the overlap run, then turning back and delivering an accurate pass. These tactics help to develop an attack which has a good chance of creating a strike at the goal. Therefore, teams trained in these patterns are less likely to blindly knock the ball into the attacking third.

Intelligent use of the overlapping player is the mark of a tactically advanced team. It is important that the entire team know why players overlap at a given moment. Usually, players overlap because they see a large empty space that can be exploited for attack; they make a long bent run at top speed. Normally, they should receive the ball for their good thinking, effort, and position.

If they get the ball, and subsequently give it up to the other team, their responsibility and commitment to that attack is usually enough to drive them to recover at speed. However, if they do not get the ball, they feel let down by their teammates, and discouraged by their waste of energy; thus, they are less likely to make a concerted recovery run.

General Coaching Point

Short passing is no more a mark of high quality soccer than long passing is a mark of poor quality soccer. Quality soccer uses a creative mixture of both short and long passes to unbalance and penetrate the defense. Short passes generally provide control, while long passes provide penetration. Too much short passing is often symptomatic of the inability to look long, or make the space required for passing far, or hit the long ball accurately.

For the goalkeeper, the situation is quite similar. The keeper needs a mixture of both long and short distribution to reach the open teammate. While the field player does not get a chance to stand, look around, and wave people away, the keeper is allowed this time to reorganize; thus there is no good excuse for a poor decision or inaccurate pass! The mindless distribution of a 30/70 long punt to a well-marked striker, or a non-penetrating pass to a wingback should not be accepted when a penetrating 70/30 pass to a midfielder would be much wiser. Like any field player, the keeper should develop accurate passes which balance possession and penetration.

15 · Alan Wade's Midfield Probing

Purpose

To maintain possession while changing the point of attack; also, to develop a team's ability to adjust its attacking style to the changes in the defense.

Exercise

This activity uses the entire field. The progression relates mainly to midfielders and backs, but the training is done with the whole team.

The first step uses short passes in developing possession and use of the full width of the field. As they move from one goal line to the other, four players pass the ball from touchline to touchline, then back again, as in the diagram. To keep full width, the two outside players must touch the touchline after every pass.

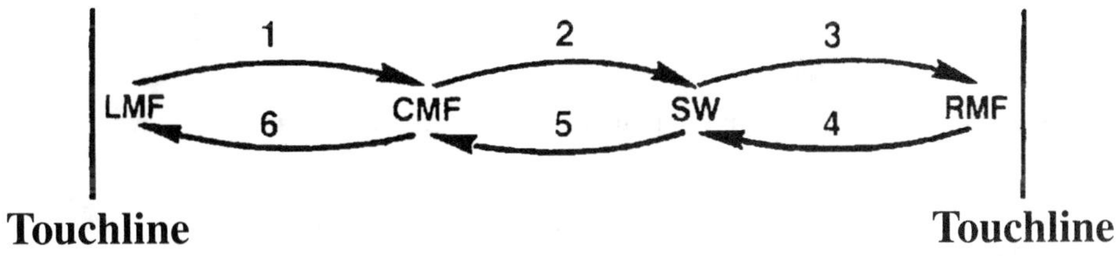

Diagram #21: Controlled change in point of attack.

Emphasize upfield vision and two-touch play, with efficient receiving and crisp passing. Some players may require three touches for the turn and service, but eventually outside players can play the ball with one touch to speed up the change in point of attack.

The second step introduces the skip pass option, which speeds up the attack. After each pass, the player must move away and be prepared for a return pass. Emphasize the importance of **each player moving toward the ball to receive it**, but outside players should move to the touchline immediately after their pass. The better players should use air balls for the skip pass, and develop proper bending of the ball.

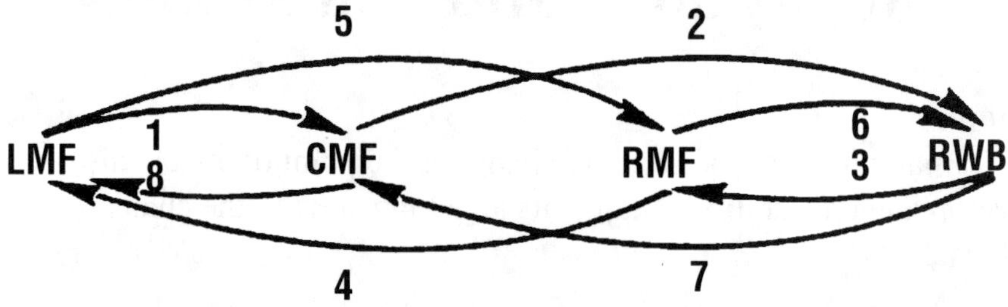

Diagram #22: Skip pass option. For the third step, introduce the layoff.

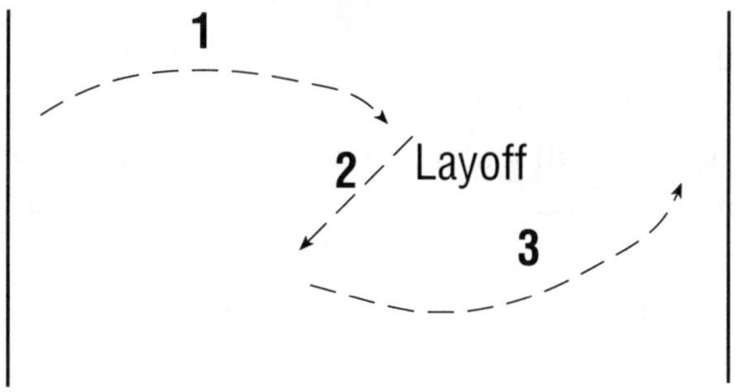

Diagram #23: Layoff; change in point of attack is generally for more accomplished players.

Here more mature players act in tandem. Obviously, with older players, service is longer, and the layoff or takeover is frequently used to aid the change in the point of attack.

The next step is a game of 11 v 6 on a full field with goalkeepers. The full side of 11 (with the keepers in EACH goal) will be the attacking team, and the small side of 6 will be the defending team. Using cones, divide the field into thirds. Place two defenders in each third, where they must remain while defending against the attacking team. Play is continuous, after attacking goal A, play merely turns around and the 11 attack goal B. There is one restriction on the attacking team, they must change fields in every third before they are allowed to shoot. A 4-4-2 configuration works well for this game.

Play begins with a shot on the full team's goal, so that the keeper can begin the attack by distribution to an open back. Younger players may need a dry run without opposition at first.

As this game is played, the coach should insist upon four man width wherever the ball is. Thus, when the ball is in the finishing third, two of the midfielders must join the forwards. This in turn demands that two midfielders move into the finishing third, which in turn requires two backs to move into the midfield area. The final strike should be made by a cross, with all three attacking slots (near post, far post, penalty area) filled.

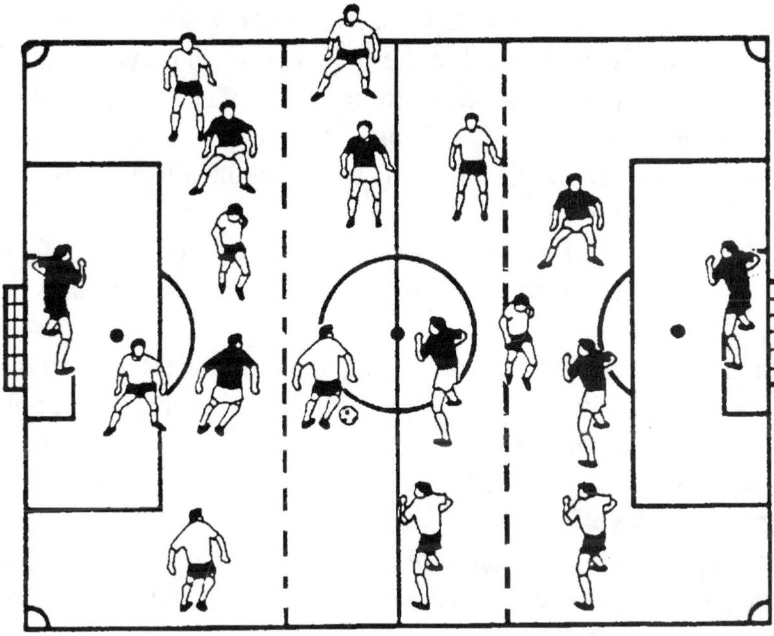

Diagram #24: Match condition changes is point of attack.

This game can be brought up to match condition by building up to 11 v 11, maintaining the emphasis on changing the point of attack in each third (at least by one team, if not both). The coach should reward every change of field. Younger teams should do this exercise with fewer players; a 3-3-2 with one defender in each third of the field works well.

During the game, not the build up exercise, the coach should instruct the "defensive" team secretly, so that the attackers will learn to look for and adjust to defensive tactical changes. Start with a low pressure defense. If the attacking team scores repeatedly, the coach should change the defensive approach to high pressure. The attack must then become more direct, with the offensive change in behavior coming from the players.

On successive penetrations by the attacking team, the coach can signal the defense to change back and forth from low to high pressure.

Discussion, Variations, Coaching Points

While the focus is on midfield play, these concepts and skills are critical to success in every third of the field and by all players. At this stage, midfield play will approach a higher level of soccer. The players will learn to observe a defensive change and adapt to it. There is no sense to rushing forward when the defense is back and the attack is given room to play in front of the defense.

Attackers will therefore seek to exploit space wherever the defense allows. At a more advanced level, some players may even create chances where none appear to exist.

A simple variation of this shortsided game eliminates marking the thirds of the field. The coach simply concentrates on changes in point of attack. This can be done by pointing out unnecessary losses of possession which could have been avoided by better support, shielding, or using square passes or layoffs as the situation warrants.

If it is necessary to use neutral players to create numbers up, by all means do so. For this exercise, an 8 v 8 game might add two neutral players who always play for the team in possession.

General Coaching Point

Adaptation to the defense and exploitation of space are the objectives in teaching systematic forward movement. Despite some claims to the contrary, a systematic attack actually encourages greater creativity. The mere elimination of confusion stimulates the imagination and the four man width promotes choice. Obviously, any system that does not have many options is restrictive. For example, no system should be so rigid as to preclude the immediate and direct counterattack as a surprise.

Systematic tactics demand a special effort by the coach, but good planning and training will enable players to attack with greater numbers and efficiency, rather than merely maintain possession. The coach must respect players who create new and different plays. Of course, this is only possible when the players can employ good technique and sound tactics. The initial premise, that players must clearly understand the basic role of first, second, and third attackers, holds true more than ever. For a thorough discussion of these basic roles, and how to use them in all aspects of soccer training, see Andrew Caruso's Soccer Coaching Development and Tactics.

16 · Palmisano's Inside-Out/Outside-In

PURPOSE

To develop a team shape for a basic system of play that will create an attack that will present many problems to the defense.

EXERCISE

Like the previous game, this activity begins as a teaching progression, and eventually uses the full field. At first, the field may need some cone grids as in the diagram.

Idealized diagrammatical sketch of the entire system.

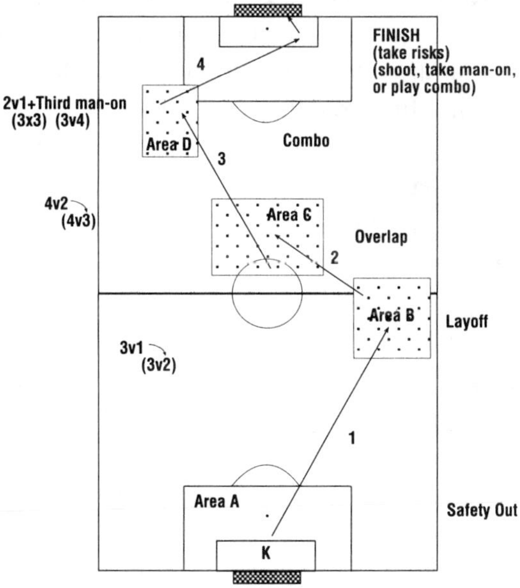

Diagram #25: Controlled changes in point of attack as shown here truly promotes scoring opportunities with reasonable chances of success.

Step 1. Keeper (area A) to Midfielders (probable layoff to defender - area B)

Step 2. Midfielders (area B) to forwards and midfielders (area C) (layoff, take over, 1 - 2 or overlap)

Step 3. Pass to Midfielders and Forwards (area C) (see the problem, midfielders constantly being named - - - this is why Defenders must be involved in attack) (area D)

Step 4. Finish (shooter dribble for shot) cross finish, or combination finish.

This overall plan is too ambitious for a single session. Therefore, consider one session for each step of the teaching progression. Practice service to each grid on successive days, using numbers shown in diagram. Then do some linking of one area to another. Each step should be done functionally; that is, at the correct locations on the field.

Emphasize the following for each step:

Step 1. Begin with a shot at the goal for keeper development and realism. Weighing the chances of possession versus penetration, the keeper should first try to get the ball to area B by a punt or a throw. At the earliest stages, the numbers in area B would be 3 v 1; then advance to 3 v 2. **With players 11-14 years old, the entire progression must be completed without defense.** Then add one passive defender in each area, then progress to a live defender.

Step 2. The pass from area B to area C gets the ball back inside, thus relieving pressure on the outside. It can be made by a midfielder or a defender who has overlapped or received a layoff. The pass should combine penetration with change of field, but it need not go beyond area C because that area provides the most options for the attack. Begin with 4 v 2 in this area, then progress to 4 v 3.

Step 3. The pass from area C to area D completes the change of field. As the defense has had to concentrate on the central area, a number of attacking options, long shots, and direct attacks become available. But usually the pass to the perimeter of the field, or better still, the perimeter of the penalty area, creates a direct shot, a tight combination, or a dangerous cross.

Step 4. In the finishing third, attackers should be encouraged to take risks, whether they shoot, dribble for a shot, cross, or combine with teammates. Begin with a 2 v 1 + a third man-on, then build to 3 v 3, and finally 3 v 4. Numbers down will force risk-taking, and simulate match conditions.

Next set up the entire grid structure, using only eleven players (shadow play) but these players must move forward to maintain the required numbers and shape. Once players can perform the entire movement (11 v 0) stringing approximately 15 passes, progress to completing the movement with 7 passes: keeper to midfielder (1); layoff to wingback (2); wingback to area C (3); layoff or takeover in area C (4); pass to overlapper in area D (5); cross (6); shot on goal (7).

Try putting as much of the entire system in place in grids with defenders, then do steps 1 - 4. Finally provide the entire movement with 11 v 4, and slowly add to the defense as successful attacks are maintained.

The shortsided play for the day emphasizes the balance of penetration with possession. The whole progression of building out of the back, controlling at midfield, and getting the ball into the attacking third under control for a quality chance to finish works best when the attacking team is constantly probing for quick penetration. Therefore, the coach should look for and point out missed opportunities for penetration, as well as mindless attempts at penetration.

Discussion, Variations, Coaching Points

This system, though it permits direct to goal options and also vertical flank play, is based upon inside-out and outside-in play. It assumes that moving the defense around is an effective penetration strategy. This demands that the attacking team maintain a shape throughout all of the movements. Allow the attackers two to five passes to maintain possession in the general area of this grid, as this may happen in a game. Of course, building the ball out of the back from the keeper to wingbacks or central defenders is an acceptable option. But reserve the long ball to the center circle or beyond for those occasions when the defense is high pressure or has moved many players up to deny building out of the back.

General Coaching Point

While some may think that progressions are only for idealists, top coaches like Bob Dikranian, one of the winningest college coaches in the U.S., use this method every session. Dikranian has used the progression method to produce great players, coaches, and referees at the youth and college level.

Use progressions, but spend 60% of your session on match related play (shortsided games) instead of 25%. More than half of any given training session should be devoted to match related and match condition activities.

17 · Quakertown's Team Shape for Youth

PURPOSE

To train players from age 7-11 in the rudiments of team shape; also to develop players' visual abilities.

EXERCISE

This progression can be done in the vicinity of the goal or in any open area. Place 11 cones on a field, simulating defender/linkmen roles and striker/linkmen roles.

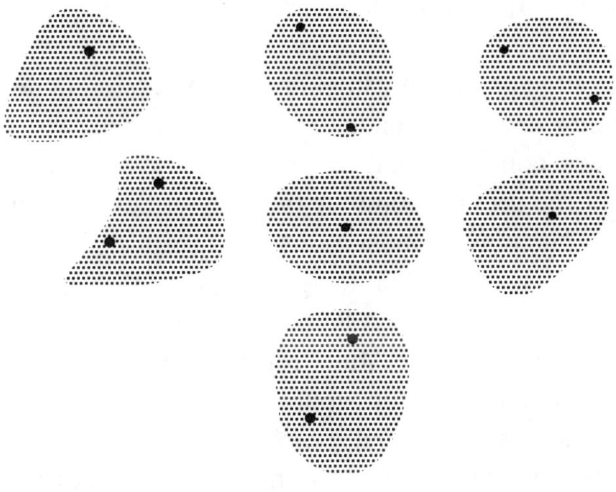

Diagram #26: This activity has many options. (see options below)

Whenever one side has no players the coach freezes the activity. If no one is up front, or no player is in the central area, obvisouly the 'team' shape is poor and the coach corrects it. Players learn this exceptionally well using this activity. Furthermore, it is then easy to get players to have good shape in both shortsided and 11 aside situations.

The basic activity uses seven attacking players, each player at a cone in each shaded area. This leaves four cones open. These players must pass the ball using two-touch play, always moving to receive the ball, then after passing the ball, moving to another open cone (generally in a different 'shaded area').

Instruct players to maintain eye contact with the ball throughout the activity. This may sometimes require bent runs, which should be encouraged. All passes and runs should be crisp and purposeful.

As soon as players are competent with the activity (possibly 3-5 minutes), add a second ball. Obviously, neither the balls nor the players should collide; nor should both balls be passed to the same player at the same time. Again eye contact is vital, not only with the ball, but with potential receivers.

The next step is to once again, use a single ball but add a defender. Keep the defenders fresh and motivated by rewarding them, such as making them part of the attacking team when they win the ball. The player who caused the turnover can become the new defender, or rotate out of the activity.

As soon as the attacking team can maintain possession under this token pressure, add a second defender, continuing to play with a single ball. Then add the second ball, and return to a single defender.

For more advanced groups, continue the progression with one ball and no defenders. The players must a) insert a takeover; b) add a 1-2 (wall pass) move; c) use a long ball (skip pass); d) If this long ball goes well, require a one-touch pass for a layoff.

Once these skills can be successfully repeated, add a defender and try a, b, and c again. The ultimate step would be for players to simultaneously use combinations and long ball passes.

Next, play a shortsided game of 4 v 4 through 6 v 6, scoring one point for a goal, three points for a combination, and five points for a goal from a combination. Correct poor team shape as necessary, but do not destroy the flow of the game.

Discussion, Variations, Coaching Points

The same shortsided game can be played with four goals instead of two. To permit success, demand that one player from the defending team stand in each of the 3-yard goals. Advanced adapted versions can be used for all ages. For example, many high school coaches use major portions of this activity and rave about results. Because so many young

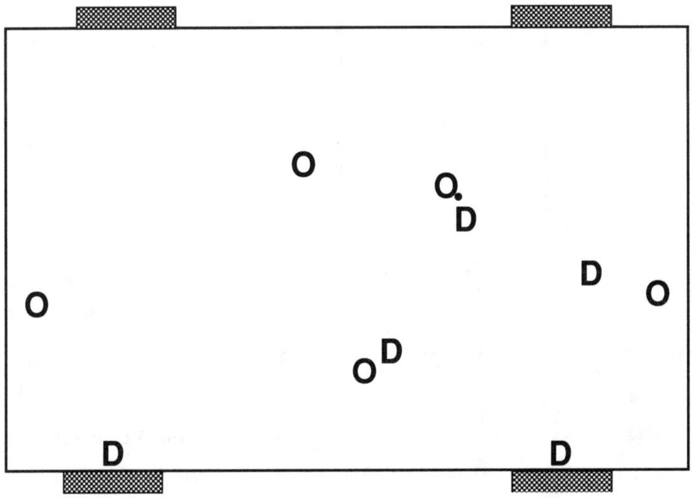

Diagram #27: Young players only know where the "cheese" (goal) is. Multiple goals helps players change point of attack and rid players of mindless linear passes. Obviously, this aides good team shape.

players begin 11 a side soccer too soon, they lack an understanding of team shape. This activity gives them this foundation.

The coach can hardly overemphasize the importance of visual (eye contact) communication with teammates at this stage of development. A related game for developing eye contact and thus moving players from the "I" stage (dribbling until they lose the ball) to the passing/receiving stage is a 2 v 2, 3 v 3, or 4 v 4 using neutral players on the side of the grid. Encourage 1-2 moves with these players. With beginners it may help to require that a player make a run to touch a perimeter cone immediately after passing the ball.

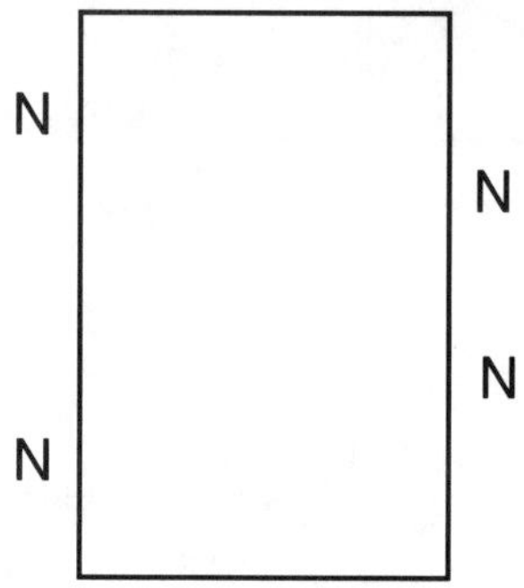

Diagram #28: This activity opens up play, creates good shape, and builds fitness.

Since this major progression is aimed at young (age 7-11) players, it may take three to five sessions of 15-25 minutes each. While the coach can and should devote some time to these more passive activities, most of the time should be spent in smallsided competitive games.

At younger (4-6) ages, some portion of the cone shape activity can be done if each player has a ball and dribbles to an open cone. This helps the very young player learn to dribble and stop, "drive" quickly in order to get to the cone first, and raise his head to look for available targets. Have fun with it, keep it moving, make a brief coaching point if a rest is needed, but keep the ball as the teacher for these young players.

For players age 7-8 who are somewhat ready to advance from the "I" stage to the passing/receiving stage, here is an excellent exercise to introduce the concept of team shape: Place 8 cones in a circle, with 6 players each at a cone. The players pass the ball and run to the vacant cone.

General Coaching Point

One of the great problems of youth soccer coaching is the teaching of positions. Young players, as well as many coaches, begin to think of positions as a place on the field or a place in relation to other players. Either concept represents a low level of understanding, because positions are (at high levels) temporary and ever-changing.

Here's why. Good soccer has many combinations (1-2's, takeovers, overlaps). All of these require that a player **leave** his or her "position." Even basic receiving techniques demands that players go to the ball; on longer passes, this could easily cause them to leave their position. On the defensive side, players often make game-saving tackles and interceptions by leaving their positions. Team shape with player **mobility** is the goal of high level successful soccer.

So coaches need to re-evaluate their thinking on teaching positions to players too young to grasp or execute these skills (generally ages 5-10). Demanding that players remain in their positions actually discourages players from going to the ball, a characteristic of all good players. This naive notion of playing a position produces low level, uncreative soccer that lacks penetration, and is therefore very simple to defend and defeat. If this were compared to a political system, it would be totalitarian: you have order without freedom.

Furthermore, the teaching of positions at this age is time-consuming and boring, with the coach talking a lot and the young players touching the ball very little and doing even less.

Obviously, this scenario is precisely the opposite of what well-intentioned coaches want to accomplish. So why does this happen? It happens because whenever you have 22 very young players on the field all chasing the ball, you have chaos. As a political system, this would of course be anarchy: freedom without order.

The question then becomes: how do we create a soccer environment that balances freedom with order? The answer involves two very practical concepts: numbers and shape. The danger of positions for ages 5-10 results from having too many players on the field. These youngsters are not proficient enough to combine with 10 teammates, and will have a difficult time learning because they will touch the ball less than 5% of the time.

The solution is therefore teams of three or four players. This eliminates positions and all the time spent in talking about them. Instead, players learn basic aspects of the game like penetration, support, mobility, delay, cover, and concentration, as well as transition. These elements are the prerequisites for positional play!

Incidentally, a full understanding of these notions is also the prerequisite of becoming a high level coach. When the coach understands first, second and third attackers and defenders responsibilities, and he can apply these notions in the confusion of a match, now he is ready to coach instead of monitor the activity. Unfortunately, acquiring such competence requires years of conscious observation of matches, as well as many hours of playing, preparing sessions, etc.

Shortsided numbers also make team shape a reality. A comprehension of team shape allows a player to understand that a position is not rigid; it may be the dominant role, but it is not the only one. Even goalkeepers can benefit from training in these environments; as they begin to understand the game, they learn to penetrate, support, and may even provide mobility at times. Furthermore, they should also provide pressure, cover and balance, much like any other player.

18 · Jim Tonrey's First Touch

PURPOSE

To develop receiving, communication, and passing skills.

EXERCISE

This activity begins as a passive exercise but becomes competitive. Use a grid that could be 20 yards square for 16 players, a little larger for more players, perhaps up to 30 yards square. This is a multiple ball activity, with one ball for every two or three players. There are no teams, no keepers, and no goals.

Place all players in the grid; they simply pass the balls among all the players, using the entire area and constantly moving.

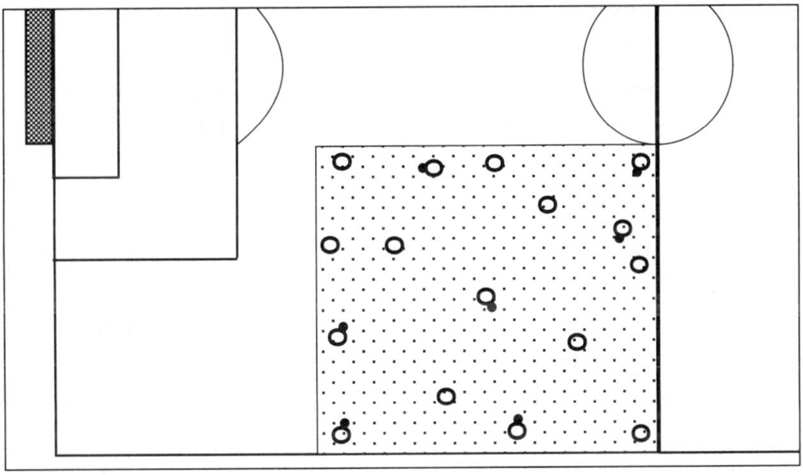

Diagram #29: This environment provides innumerable options. Here we show 16 players with 7 balls.

As soon as players can execute this first step simply passing and moving **using the entire grid**, demand good changes of pace, sharp acceleration, and full vision of the field. Continue to look for these habits, while adding specific demands, depending on players' ability.

For example,

1. eye contact before every pass;
2. accelerated run to call for ball;
3. always move toward every pass (this requires properly paced passes);
4. get the entire body behind the pass;
5. turn away from pressure (the nearest player can be considered a defender;
6. a dribble past the nearest "defender";
7. add several defenders carrying scrimmage vests (whenever they win the ball, they switch with attacker);
8. pass only with the inside of the foot (or outside, instep, or weaker foot);
9. use a specified number of touches (1, 2, or 3);
10. send and receiving air balls;
11. pass to the player who is farthest away;
12. combine with another player (1-2, takeover, overlap);
13. open the hips toward where players are for every reception;
14. divide into two or more teams, add a second ball, and have teams try to possess two balls at a time.

Try no more than five or six variations in a given day, but keep focused on one which is your main objective. Then move on to a shortsided game that emphasizes first touch, especially those skills that you focused on for this session. Generally, use full-size goals on a field size appropriate to the restrictions involved.

Discussion, Variations, Coaching Points

When you first try this activity, do not get discouraged with the results; even experienced college coaches find significant improvement after coaching this exercise two or three times.

This activity has great flexibility, involves much ball contact, and can be done often because there are so many possible variations and themes. One of those themes could be communication, which is more than just talk. It includes hand signals, body movement, posture, acceleration, and eye contact. A good wrinkle is to emphasize all communication **except** talk. Some talk is actually destructive! Always discourage negative talk, which destroys confidence and focus, and calling for the ball when not open, which causes turnovers. Talk is still important, but the major communication weakness usually lies in these other areas.

This is also a good time for banter, verbal fun, building team morale, and even developing psychological strength. For the latter, ask players to visualize themselves in the game, constantly receiving and turning from pressure to successfully complete a pass.

Fitness can be emphasized by merely reducing the number and amount of time used for coaching points. Generally, at this time it becomes appropriate to use lots of verbal encouragement to keep players working hard. Since this is a matter of coaching style, it is neither good nor bad in itself, and not necessarily recommended for all coaches.

General Coaching Point

A type of communication that is often misunderstood and even abused is the coach's communication with the referee. Many coaches believe that "working the ref" is a winning strategy, but the fact is that this tactic has lost many more games than it has ever won. This unhealthy behavior causes teams to believe that the referee determines the final result.

In games of parity or near parity, the team's effort generally determines the final result. Great coaches know this, so they work hard to influence their team's efforts. That is why so many great coaches are above the self-defeating tactic of working the referee. They and their players excel when they focus on the game and not the referee.

19 · John Elliff's Target Penetration

Purpose

To develop attacking skills using an offense with one or two strikers.

Exercise

This is another progression which begins as a teaching session and builds into a shortsided game. Use the attacking third of the field with the strikers, adding midfielders and defenders as training progresses. Rehearse one of the following attacking patterns with these three or four players while the rest of the team is engaged in some form of keep away (4 v 2, etc.). Then these three or four players could show the rest of the team what they have rehearsed.

With two strikers, as in a 4-4-2 or 3-5-2 configuration, these two front line players should play in tandem as opposed to side by side. The coach should know the characteristics of each striker. The player furthest forward is usually very strong, capable in the air, able to shield, dribble, combine, assist, and of course, score. The second striker may not match up to the first physically, but he or she generally is quick to read and anticipate the game, creative, and very capable of laying the ball off and playing combinations.

Once you have found your strikers, teach them to play in tandem, all the time adjusting their positions to exploit space. Usually they will both gravitate to the ball side of the field.

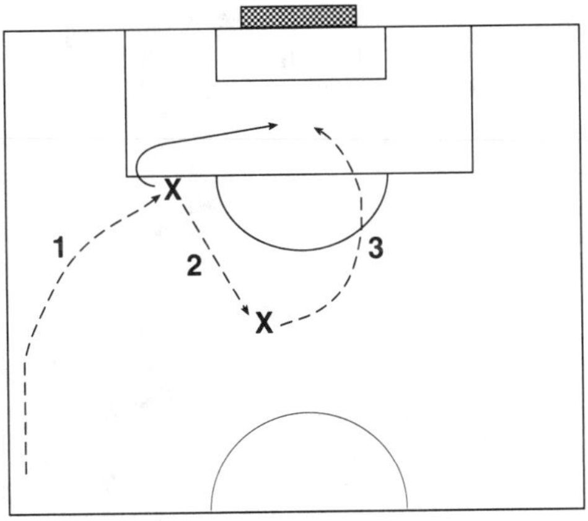

Diagram #30: Players need to take some risks in order to score. Here a pass to the player nearest the goal opens many possibilities for the attack. The target player has laid the ball off to the other striker and has spun around to receive a chip for a shot on goal. The spin should be on the blind side of the defender.

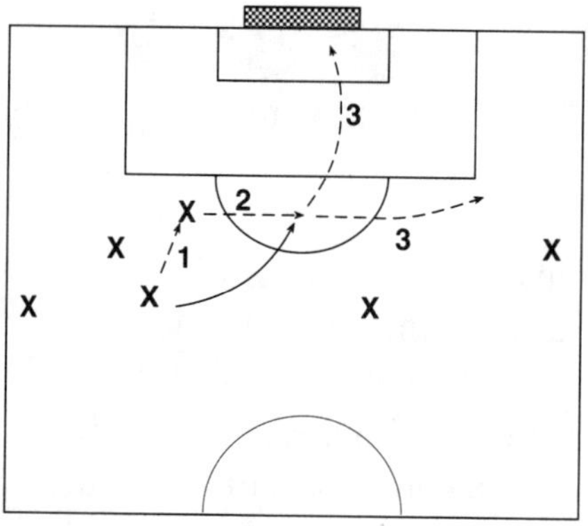

Diagram #31: Wall passes are always trouble for the defense. In this case the target player has played a **1-2** (wall pass) with a central midfielder. The same play could be done with nearly any other player on the field. In any case, the result could be a pass to a third man on, a shot, or even a return pass.

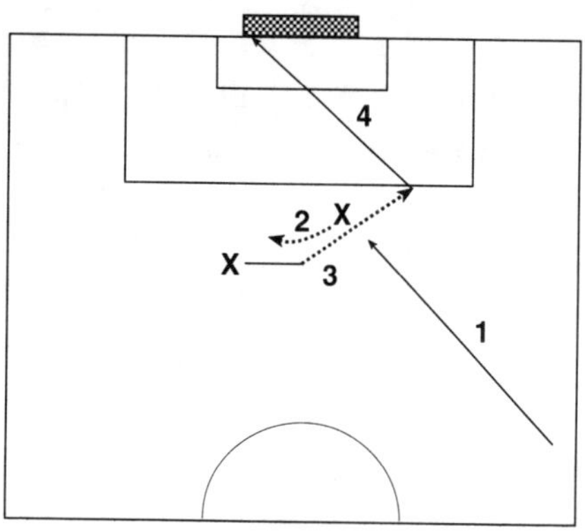

Diagram #32: Takeovers in this area create excellent opportunities for strikes on goal. Here the target player has received the ball, and **dribbled left to create a takeover** with the other striker, resulting in a shot on goal. This is a very effective weapon against the offsides trap; the confusion caused by the takeover creates a shooting opportunity. (This play was often seen in the former NASL.)

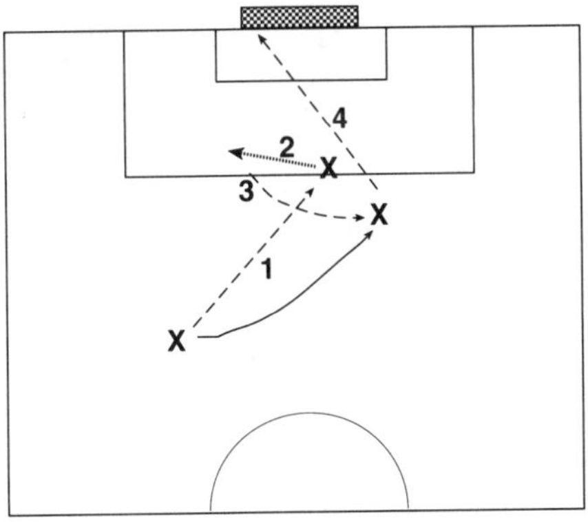

Diagram #33: Shown here is a return pass to the server. Even a sideways dribble in this area can create defensive confusion. Here the target player has received the ball and penetrated somewhat with a dribble to the left. As the defense moves to cover, the attacker can lay the ball off to an oncoming third player. Another option would be a double pass back to the server, or service to an outside overlap. The shortsided game of the day should emphasize the particular pattern rehearsed. To encourage repeated tries, score three points for goals which resulted from specific movement that was taught.

Discussion, Variations, Coaching Points

Remember to concentrate on only one of the patterns during a session. After about four sessions of these various patterns, a whole session could possibly be devoted to using **all** the movements in a single shortsided game to full size goals. Begin with a brief (less than ten minutes) review, then play the shortsided game for 45-60 minutes, with short water breaks.

General Coaching Point

The necessity for ending practice sessions with at least 15 minutes of totally uncoached and uninterrupted playing time has been emphasized. But this should not be construed as idle time for the coach or parent monitor. If the coach is present, this vital part of practice allows time to carefully observe, refine diagnosis, and create fun environments that will help player development. If a parent monitor is running the session, he or she never coaches above his or her knowledge; the parent monitor, therefore, relies on the ball, game, player, and environment to teach the game. It is far better to allow the game to teach rather than to interrupt to make an incorrect coaching point.

One must recall, the game and the ball has produced thousands of professional players for decades, many who had virtually no coaching until age 14, 15, 16 or older.

20 · Sarah Ferland & Meghan Cepetelli's Finishing School

PURPOSE

To develop finishing skills in a fun environment.

EXERCISE

This is a 1 v 1 v 1 v K, which is done in a long, narrow area with cones and goals arranged as in the diagram below.

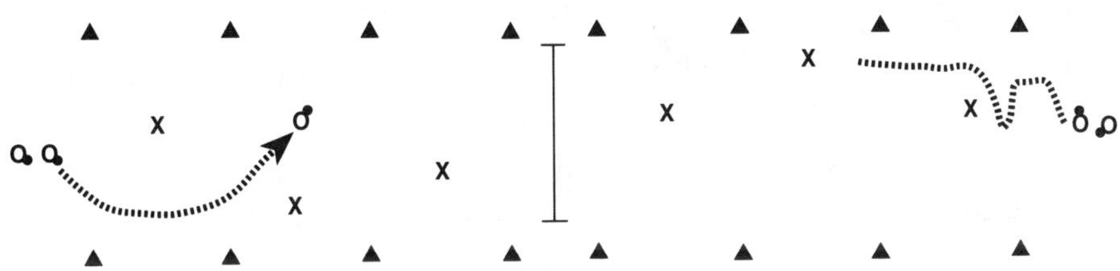

Diagram #34: Taking people on while continuing toward the goal creates a strong attacking mentality.

The cones define the limits for each defender, who may not go out of that area. An attacker dribbles to beat each defender successively, then shoots on a full-size goal and keeper. Defenders may have to be limited in some cases; for example, younger players may require defenders to play in the crab position. But goalkeepers should play 100%, assuming that they have had proper training and a thorough warm-up.

With two keepers, four defenders, and only eight shooters on one Coerver goal (using both sides of the goal), this activity can move along quickly, with no one waiting in line. When an attacker reaches the second grid, the next attacker can begin. Rotate defenders through each grid every minute or so then they can become attackers.

Follow this activity with a shortsided game using full-size goals and goalkeepers. In the beginning stage, placing some number or space limitation on the defenders may help the attackers create many shooting opportunities. But with advanced teams, match conditions often require that the attackers be outnumbered by the defenders.

Another shooting game with full-size goals and keepers that allows for many repetitions and full competitiveness involves dividing up the players into two teams of equal numbers. On each team, players are given numbers. Each team lines up an equal distance from the goal. The coach stands off to the side or near midfield with a good supply of balls. As the coach throws or rolls a ball into the field of play, he or she calls out one or more numbers. Those players from each team with these numbers sprint to the ball; the first team to control the ball becomes the attacking team, while the other team defends. The shot should be taken at the earliest possible opportunity. If the ball goes out of bounds, start the next group immediately.

The coach can determine how long these teams should play; until a goal is scored, a shot is stopped by the keeper, or a given amount of time has elapsed. If the keeper needs throwing or punting practice, play can continue until the keeper has sent the ball back to a target player at midfield or beyond.

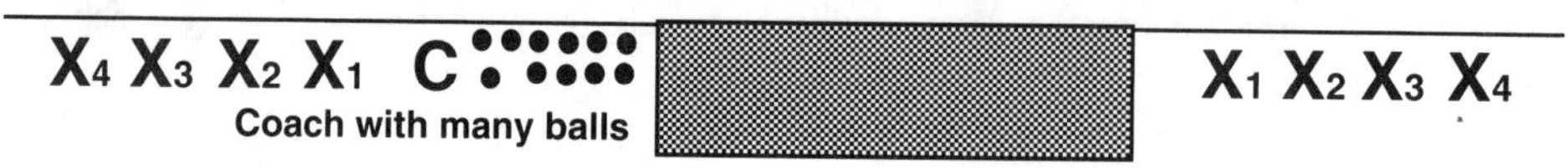

Diagram #35: Having 1 v 1 dribbling battles with as many as 4 players at a time mixes dribbling and passing/receiving skills in a realistic tactical situation.

Coaches should vary their services to begin this game, mixing short passes, long balls, high balls, bouncing balls, etc. Keeping score encourages full effort, but discourage defensive fouls.

A major wrinkle to this game is to use designated attacking and defending teams, as in the diagram below. Shannon (Higgins) Cervoski uses this activity with great success at George Washington University.

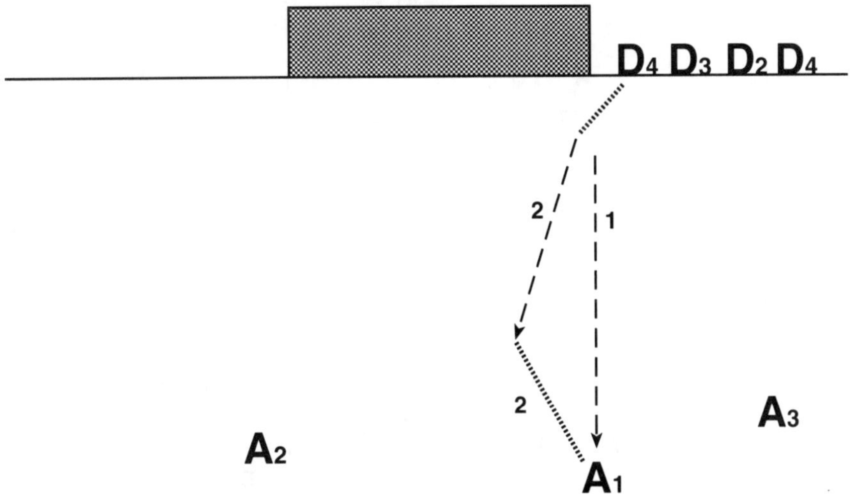

Diagram #36: Server dribbles to penalty spot, serves to attacker, then immediately pressures that attacker, trying to deny an immediate shot.

The pivotal exercise in the progression involves four attackers and up to four defenders on half a field. All attackers are well outside the penalty area. Three defenders start from the goal line, and the fourth defender serves from the penalty spot. When the ball is served to an attacker, the server immediately becomes the first defender and closes from the first attacker. With each pass, another defender is allowed to come off the goal line and pressure the attack. Thus, if three passes are made, the game becomes a 4 v 4; if only one pass is made, it is 4 v 2. Each round ends with a shot from either team. The defense can shoot on two small goals spaced widely apart at midfield.

To maintain a match-related environment, keep score. Allow the defense two points for denying a shot on goal. Allow the attack one point for every shot on goal, and two points for a goal scored.

This next game, called Holahan's Gate Keeper, also uses full-size goals and keepers. Divide players into two teams, stationed on the end line on either side of the goal. Each player has a ball. At the coach's signal, the first player on each team dribbles through a cone obstacle course to a gate, about twenty yards away. The first player through the gate becomes the attacker, while the other player immediately abandons his or her ball to become the defender.

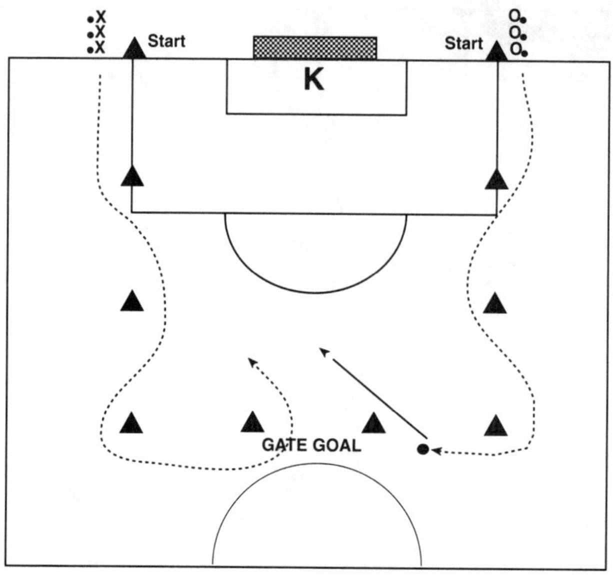

Diagram #37: Players request to play this game again and again.

The defender can win the ball, shoot, and score. Each individual game ends with a shot on goal or an out-of-bounds ball. (The obstacle cones can also serve as the boundary lines.)

Keep score.

To keep the game moving quickly, start the next two players as soon as the first player gets through the gate.

Since destruction is always easier than construction, adjust the scoring and/or teams so that attack and defense are close in score. To keep focused on coaching, some coaches simply let their players keep score, but this is just a matter of personal preference.

The key to both the fun and the development in these games is to keep them moving quickly. Groups of twelve to twenty players require two groups. Since there are short periods of waiting time, this presents the opportunity to coach players as they rest, get a drink, or wait their turn.

Demand that the players follow their shots, and give 100% to these games. For some sessions, create specific parity match-ups, so that the same two players compete against each other the whole time. Most of the time, however, random match-ups are fine.

Discussion, Variations, Coaching Points

These games can be adapted in any number of ways to create specific challenges:

1. No keeper;
2. Keeper cannot use hands (this develops footwork);
3. Defender must keep hand behind back;
4. A neutral player helps the attacker (encourages 1-2):
5. Defender(s) must count out loud ("one-thousand-one, one-thousand-two" etc.) to 6 before playing;
6. A single cone or gate to "drive" through instead of controlled dribble;
7. Move the gate goal closer or further than the usual twenty yards;
8. Double the number of players involved in each round, thus creating 2 v 2, 4 v 4, etc.

Every coach needs fun activities that provide abundant finishing under match conditions. As in match play, time-wasting and excessive passing in the box result in lost opportunities. Players love these activities, because scoring goals is still the ultimate challenge in developing attractive soccer.

General Coaching Point

Allow players to contribute to the training sessions. The first time you ask them for input, they may not be likely to respond. Simply wait 30 seconds or more until someone does contribute. If not, direct a question to a specific player who is not likely to be intimidated. For example, "John, what do you think was useful about today's workout?" Understand that children may not be accustomed to this approach.

Having asked such a question, the coach must be willing to give the fullest, most respectful attention to any response.

Another way that players can contribute is to have them conduct fragments of the training session. This is best done with advance planning. Also encourage players to referee scrimmages and larger shortsided games. This will teach them another phase of the game as well as sensitize them to the challenge of refereeing. It may even avoid a red card someday when you really need eleven players. In the long run, such measures help produce better referees and players.

Sometimes injured players are not capable of training, but are capable of these roles. It gives them something to do, makes them feel useful, and helps bond the team.

21 · Bobby Clark's Cover The Essence of Defense

PURPOSE

To develop the roles of first defender (which is pressure) and second defender (which is cover), thus improving all team defense, whether it is man-to-man or zone.

EXERCISE

The first exercises are 1 v 1 games that focus on the first defender and the role of pressure. Use grids of approximately twenty yards, with four cone goals, one in the middle of each line. Two players stand in each of these goals. To begin, one player will serve the ball across the grid to another player, who becomes the attacker. The server becomes the defender, moving fast while the ball is traveling, but closing in at a slower speed. The attacker attempts to score on the server's goal, while the server attempts to steer the attacker to one side.

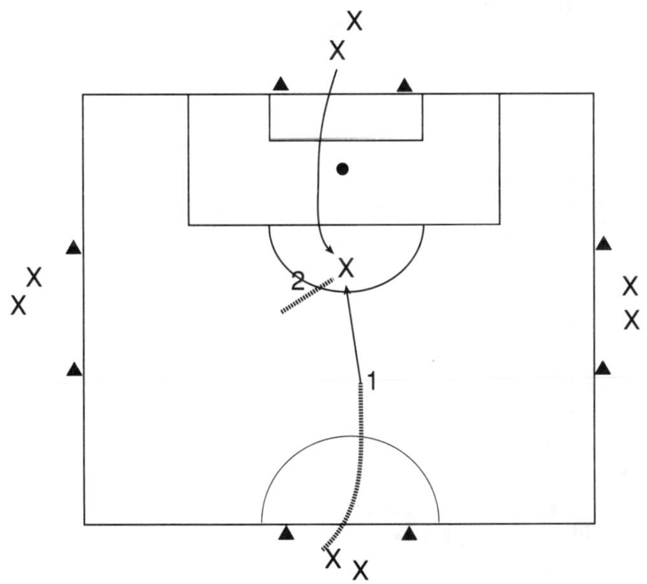

Diagram #38: Basic format for various 1 v 1, 1 v 2, and 2 v 2 activities. Cone goals are approximately 3 yards wide.

Alternate service in a crisscross fashion so that each player takes several turns as both attacker and defender.

The next step gives the defensive role to the partner in the same goal as the receiver. The server sends the ball across the grid, but this time the defender comes from the same location as the attacker. The attacker attempts to turn and score on his or her "own" goal, while the defender attempts to deny the turn.

If the defender can deny any turn for six seconds, he or she has essentially been successful; however, play continues until the attacker turns or the defender wins the ball.

The next activity uses the same grid, or perhaps a slightly larger one, for a 1 v 2 game that develops the role of the second defender. The server and his or her partner become the defenders. While the first defender applies pressure, the second supplies cover. The coach can focus on distance, angle, timing, vision, body position, recovery, or communication. But always emphasize defensive success as the result of hard work, a competitive disposition, and not letting yourself get beat.

In the same grid, or a slightly larger rectangular grid, the game can progress to a 2 v 2, still emphasizing the defensive roles and communication between defenders.

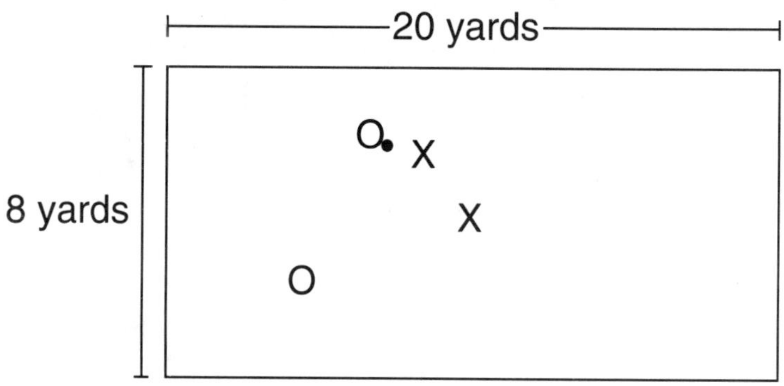

Diagram #39: 2 v 2 provides great technical, tactical, fitness and psychological development.

The rigorous demands of 2 v 2 require frequent stoppages. Provide a one minute rest every two to three minutes, making adjustments for the fitness of your players. The break allows time for water, a quick demonstration or coaching point to correct errors or point out strengths.

Continue to build the defensive roles with a 4 v 2 in a tight grid, just small enough to challenge your players. For high school varsity players, a ten yard grid is about right; for less able players, allow more space.

In this standard game, the attackers score a point for every ten consecutive passes and two points for every pass that splits the defenders. The defenders score a point every time they win the ball. Rotate two new defenders in every two or three minutes.

With the six players involved in the 4 v 2, it is easy to move to a short-sided game of 3 v 3. Use a grid approximately 30 by 15 yards with goals about two yards wide. To keep play from becoming sloppy, use brief stoppages for instruction and questions. Stay extremely focused on problems of **cover** avoiding the temptation to deal with attack.

Discussion, Variations, Coaching Points

Inexperienced coaches often teach man-to-man defense. While strict man-to-man is easily taught, it is more easily beaten by well-coached opponents. Man-to-man defense creates a chain of 1 v 1 contests, where mismatches are inevitably exploited by good attackers. Furthermore, the game creates numerous 3 v 2 and 2 v 1 situations; when the man-to-man defense is outnumbered, it can become totally ineffective.

Quality defense requires a knowledge of man-to-man marking skills plus a knowledge of zonal skills, particularly cover. Effective defenses can both mark well and play zonally to provide cover. Novice coaches should allow the game to carry the experience. This is a good time for the coach or parent monitor to learn more about cover by **observing**.

Young players often have good insights in regard to cover, but frequently instructions from parents and coaches destroy this good intuition.

At higher coaching levels, the obvious prerequisite to teaching defensive cover is that the first defenders know how to put pressure on the ball so that the second defender can properly assist. When there is no cover, the first defender must be extremely patient, concentrating on delaying the attack by, 1) keeping play in front of the defense, 2) seeing the ball and the attacker, 3) not getting beat, 4) trying to prevent the attacker from turning towards goal, and if that fails, 5) steering the attacker away from penetration. Against a superior player, when all else fails, the first defender should at least try to, 6) make the attacker predictable. All of these skills involve maintaining a proper distance and angle to the attacker.

When cover is present, the first defender, depending on other circumstances, can be much more aggressive, trying to steal the ball, poke tackle, and make serious, but not reckless, attempts to win the ball or at least force the attacker to keep his or her head down to maintain possession.

Teaching cover, the role of the second attacker, not only takes time, but requires a solid understanding of support, the role of the second attacker. Especially in the 2 v 2, teach attack before defense, support before cover. Furthermore, focus on only one aspect of the game at a time.

Although diagrams and chalk talk may help, actual field demonstration and walk-throughs solidify the various concepts of distance. The subtleties of cover make it especially difficult to communicate in book form; however, the key concepts for cover include:

1. Helping the first defender; this includes knowing when to double and when to hang back, and avoiding too much commitment to a player who does not have the ball;
2. providing depth to a defense, positioning to cut out passes instead of marking;
3. helping to balance the defense, even though we usually assign balance to the third defender,
4. communicating on all those issues.

Again, shortsided games can be used to teach these concepts. Freezes must be very sharp because good cover and poor cover can vary as little as a yard or two, a decision made half a second too late, or an angle that is only slightly off. Attempt to focus on how a given team could have denied a score by using cover more effectively.

In any case, neither man-to-man nor zone defense can be effective without players who understand cover. Many leading American coaches consider this the biggest weakness of all player roles. An often told anecdote describes the literal-minded man-to-man defender who was instructed to follow his opponent no matter what; so late in the game, the young defender follows his opponent off the field to the water jug. It's a cute story, but when that opponent's teammate scores, it loses its humor and points out that our young defender might have prevented the goal had he understood the notion of cover. This anecdote is even more depressing when the young defender is 15 years old.

General Coaching Point

There is nothing innately wrong with being a novice. American soccer would be nowhere without the thousands of novices who provide a soccer environment for our youth. With the proper environment, both the players and the beginner coach can learn from the game itself. This requires an open mind! Rather than pretending to be an expert, the new coach would do well to ask questions of players, and carefully listen to their responses. It is dangerous to coach beyond one's knowledge; instead of correcting, altering, or elaborating, try to gain new insights into the game and the players. Both the novice and the veteran will accomplish more through enthusiasm and honesty than by pretending to know everything about the game.

One way for any coach to show enthusiasm is to arrive early to practice with a complete written plan and training equipment: water, complete first aid kit, portable goals with nets, scrimmage vests, cones, extra soccer balls, medicine balls, pump with needle, keeper shirt and gloves, sunscreen, etc. This list may seem formidable at first; but once you begin to obtain the necessary equipment, your training sessions and player performance will be more fun and productive. For club coaches the entire team should fund these purchases.

22 · Barry Gorman's Shootout

Purpose

To develop attack, emphasizing the taking of available opportunities and getting the ball on goal.

Exercise

The first level is match related, but quickly moves to match condition with a keeper and defender. Start with a keeper and two strikers. One is a target player just inside the penalty area, while the other serves the ball off a dribble. The server dribbles from the center circle, passes to the target player; the target lays off the ball to the server who shoots on goal.

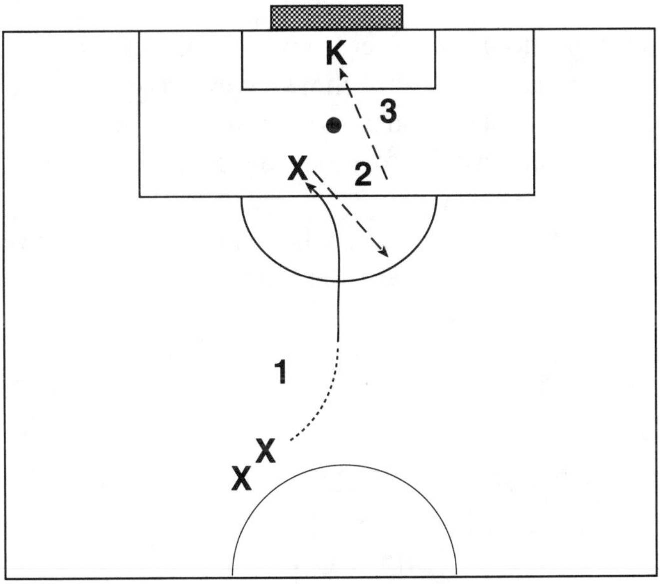

Diagram #40: This activity encourages shooting at the first opportunity. Too many touches in the penalty area are usually unproductive. On alternate occasions the layoff can be a wall pass.

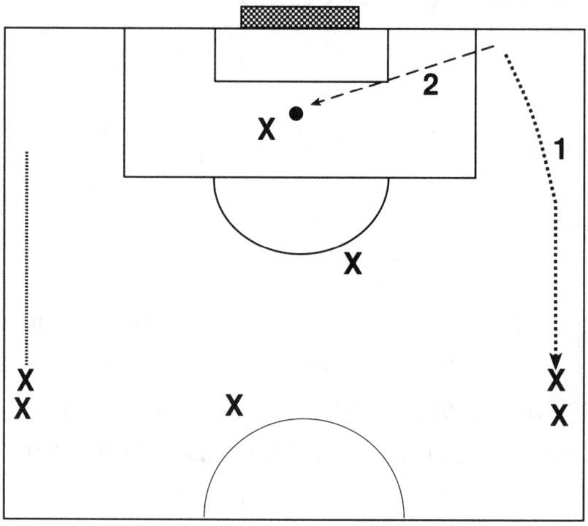

Diagram #41: Layoffs and balls pulled back from the goal line give defenders a great deal of trouble.

The second step is to use a server from each attacking corner. After the first shot (as above), another ball is immediately served from one corner, then the other. The two strikers try to finish all three opportunities as expediently as possible. After a few tries, the coach can demand one-touch shots.

The third step is to add a defender who holds a scrimmage vest in his hand to identify himself. This starts the full rotation: server/shooter to target player, target player to defender, defender to left corner, left corner to right corner, and finally, right corner to server/shooter.

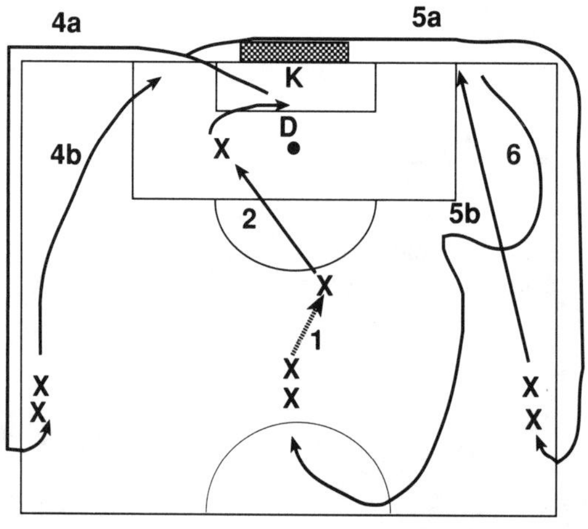

Diagram #42: This is a super shooting activity.

Discussion, Variations, Coaching Points

Keep this exercise moving quickly. If there are two keepers, let them alternate for every attack. When keepers win the ball, they might distribute to the next attacking player, or to another target player.

Emphasize the importance of timing for the attackers. Slots should be attacked running at speed at the correct time.

General Coaching Point

The ball is a fine teacher, even without the coach. Therefore, avoid all manner of standing around on the part of players. As a progression or exercise begins, use more than one group whenever possible. If not, have uninvolved players do something appropriate, perhaps 1 v 1, or 3 v 1, or a particular skill that will be required in that particular session.

23 · Center Lane Neutrals (6 v 4 + 2N)

Purpose

To provide vital play on the perimeter of the field, and to develop good support through intelligent and creative use of space.

Exercise

This activity uses neutral players in a single lane down the middle of the playing area, while the **active players are wide**.

While numbers may vary, this game works best with players from age 11-16 when the attacking team outnumbers the defenders (without counting the neutral players). Use one half of a field, marking a lane down the center approximately 15 yards wide. Only the neutral players are permitted in this lane.

Use a full-size goal for the attackers, and two small goals for the defenders. The attacking team, usually having numbers up, attempts to score on the full-size goal, while the defenders may shoot on either of two small goals placed on either side of the center circle.

Begin with a 4 v 1 + 1N, build to 4 v 2 + 1N, and finally 6 v 4 + 2N. Always add the attacking players first. The neutral players should move within their lane in order to offer proper support at all times. But do not encourage the use of these neutrals except to maintain possession. The neutrals cannot score.

Score one point for a goal, one point for 10 passes, and three points for goal after 10 passes. If defenders win the ball they get one point and a score on the small goals counts 5 points. Next, remove the neutral players and their lane restriction and play a game of 6 v 4, 7 v 5, or 8 v 5 depending on the number of players available. With age 11-12, a game of 8 v 4 may be required. Finally, add a keeper to the large goal. After players become very accomplished, play with equal numbers still demanding full use of the area provided.

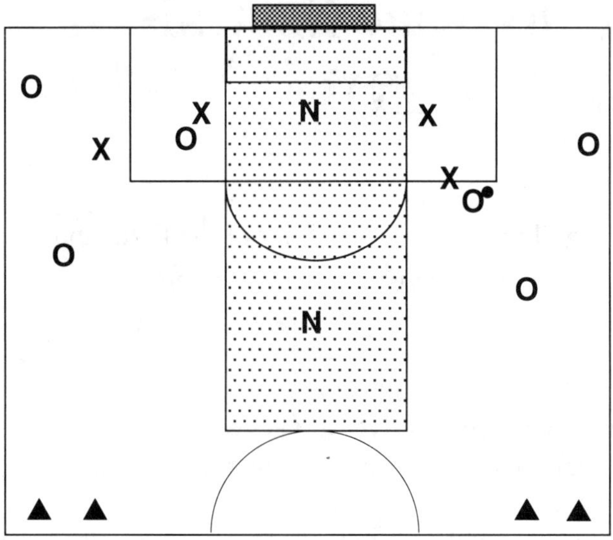

Diagram #43: Only the neutrals are permitted in the center lane.

Discussion, Variations, Coaching Points

One of the major tactical problems of soccer is the use of space. Since young players do not readily use the width of the field, placing neutral players in lanes on these flanks causes players to pass there. But it does not always solve the more fundamental problem of getting players to think and play with the full width of the field. With the **active players wide**, the exercise is very functional. This game demands the use of the perimeter of the field for safe penetration.

While direct attacks are acceptable and common nowadays, it is still good for players to use the perimeters of the field and to cross the ball. This activity is fun, competitive, economical, and does in fact lead to better use of the field.

For players ages 14 and up, the activity can be 4 v 4 with 2 neutrals. Then remove the neutrals and simply play 4 v 4. Obviously, this is a possession and change in point of attack activity; therefore, support is an integral component.

To emphasize other aspects, restrictions can be imposed. For example, to encourage combination play, require a specific play before scoring; i.e., ten passes, a change in point of attack, or a combination involving a third player.

Other options include removing the area restriction for the neutrals or using equal numbers, before finally removing all restrictions.

General Coaching Point

While direct play is a matter of style, choice, and personal preference for adult teams, in younger teams it inevitably deteriorates to kick and run. This, accompanied by the all-too-common emphasis on winning, delays player development. Therefore, for youth, a controlled style emphasizing possession, passing, receiving, and combination play should precede direct play. Once players have achieved a sense of control of the ball and basic possession tactics, more direct styles become both acceptable and effective.

This is appropriate sideline behavior. Inspite of 2 soft goals and a great rivalry with North Carolina the University of Virginia bench remained composed and professional.

Great facilities help the game in every way, but it especially helps individual performances, high level team tactics and spectator enjoyment.

Old rivalries for a 'new' game. Chris Malone, Cortland State on left and Pat Farmer, Ithaca, prepare to do battle in NCAA tourney match. Conditions were meant for courageous players and intense rivalries. This caliber existed in N.Y. State for decades. Both coaches have won National Championships. Pat Farmer is now developing 'new' rivalries at Penn State.

Here neutral players on the flanks help wing attacking play. Once players gain confidence the neutral ground is removed and teams play with equal numbers. These shortsided games to full size goals are imperative.

Lightweight regulation World Champion ball is now widely used by men and women. Anson's most remarkable asset is his continuous ability to learn from anyone or any situation, and of course his eagerness to teach (share) what he has learned. His success is not an accident, but a result of excellence.

While we have Tony Waiters to thank for proliferating 3 v 3, we must also learn the values of 2 v 2, 4 v 4, 1 v 1, 3 v 2 and all manner of shortsided play. Multiple goals for players should be a regular part of any training. The little 'tikes' (ages 5-50) frequently only know where the cheese is, therefore to elicit certain behaviors we must constantly arrange the cheese in order to accomplish our training goals.

A constant learner, we have Jeff Tipping to thank for the raising of the levels of consciousness and importance of zonal play. A true leader. While we make jokes about man-to-man and youngsters going off the field because they are marking so intently, the humor is greatly lost when a youngster 14 or more years old actually does this.

College roommates and teammates reunite after thirty-four years. Some guys never know when to quit. But then again, why quit?

Mentors are a rare and wonderful occurance. Chris Sweeney, All-American Cortland, N.Y. State Staff coach for many years got me to understand the essence of youth soccer. This unlikely crew could play with anyone along the eastern seaboard; winners of many tournaments and league titles. This is a 95 degree day preparing for a California education in soccer.

Big Jack Charlton with my friend Frank Loris, look alikes at World Cup 1994. Personalities like Jack are imperative to the game. I didn't feel that way in the opening game at the Meadowlands against Italy in World Cup 1994.

Shawn MacDonald ('A' level course roommate) who never sleeps . . . no wonder it took several chances for me to get through the 'A' course. Shawn asks Tabarez, Uraguay's National Coach, "you really mean we're suppose to have fun?" Tabarez had just spent 2 hours emphasizing the fun games approach.

The World Champion greatly encourages quality heading technique and removes fear. It adds beauty to the game because there is nothing pretty about a player (male or female) converting a head ball into a chest collection. Here Anson Dorrance, at a press conference, points out the advantages of the ball. The fact that he has my brother Vinnie interested in soccer is testimony to Anson's entertaining ability.

Coerver moves and methods are sometimes described as circus activity, but only by those who never spent any significant time with Wiel. No one has more ways to put dribbling into shortsided games and to make dribbling functional.

Coaches need to have fun! Jape Shattuck and NSCAA staff enjoy a relaxing social after a 2 day curriculum development symposium in Allentown. A welcome change, two outstanding female coaches contributed.
Top to bottom: Ron Ost, Shellas Hyndman, Leslie Gallimore, Karen Stanley and Jape.

The flamboyant Julio Mazzei of Brazil, at N.Y. City World Cup venue sites press conference. Cosmos coach, TV announcer, clinician, speaker, deliverer of Pele´ to U.S., but most of all, entertainer. Just a breath of fresh air!

Quinn's game approach has probably never been better implemented than it is by Nick Megalodis and Tom Mulroy of Soccer Educational Services of Miami. They know how to combine fun and skills development both on and off the field.

Enzo Scifo, the consummate midfielder, at World Cup practice. In smallsided games, Scifo regularly plays over 40 minutes without losing the ball. He knows the value of working hard in practice.

Left to Right: Walt Chyzowych, Carmine Tramantozzi, and Sandra Mazzola the director of soccer for Italy. Sandra focused on Italian National team training sessions which always begin with simple fun games with many ball touches. We all listened in amazement that $1,000,000 a year plus players must have fun in order to perform in a peak manner.

Ralph Lundy and Ralph Polson's camps exemplify quality and the fun games approach to development. Camps are a significant component of player youth development in the U.S.

Local telecasts like this will eventually help to develop quality commentators on a National level, thereby improving soccer spectatorship, attendance and enjoyment.

How's this for a mug shot? The Soccer Industry Council of America (SICA) All Stars Challenge the Tampa Bay Rowdies. Rodney Marsh (above) started for the Rowdies, need I say anymore about the result? These are the types of events that are more common in soccer Nations -- we're getting there quickly.

Bobby Clark, Scottish International formally of Dartmouth, now National Coach in New Zealand. Brilliant, modest and personable. Many hope to see his return to the U.S. and National involvement. I like to think I choose my mentors well!

No one more clearly exemplifies humor and athletic appreciation of the game than our frequent visitor and friend from Scotland, Andy Roxborough. Here he is serving as technical advisor for FIFA at World Cup 1994.

Doug May, Jeff Tipping, Ron McEachen and Jimmy Lenox, my first licensing instructors. Lenox was emphatic that no session should take place without shooting to full-sized goals in a match condition environment. I believed it then, and NOW!

Here two keepers face off practicing saving and distributing line drives to the other goal net. We need to have keepers do much more in the net, involving decision making. Emphasis should be on crosses, breakaways, location for special situations, communication and distribution. There is far too much time spent out of goal on isolated technical instruction.

This coach clearly recognizes the value that no session should ever take place without a goal net.

The essence of training sessions for the Dutch National Team is smallsided games using small goals at first, then progressing to full-size goals. I was thrilled to be at their World Cup Florida practice.

As more players' become referee's the level of officiating can only improve.

One of the great features of soccer is that it is a worldwide phenomenon. Travel, friendships and education are virtually part of the game.

Mike Berticelli, Notre Dame head coach, gives a clinic on goalkeeping at Muhlenburg. Mike focused on the goal, and as usual entertained as he educated.

While street soccer is slowly growing, all U.S. experts recognize the need for 'pickup games' and independent play. At the very least there is some independent play, wall kicking, juggling etc., slowly creeping into the fabric of American Soccer. We know that visualization and imagination in these situations are critical to the development of a great player.

24 · Penn State Half Field Scrimmage

PURPOSE

To develop possession, change in point of attack, use of target players and width in the attack.

EXERCISE

Use 1/3 to 1/2 of the field. Play 5 v 5 with a keeper in goal and two neutral players who always play with the team in possession. Generally, the neutrals are limited to two touches at a time. The two neutrals are restricted to two consecutive passes with each other.

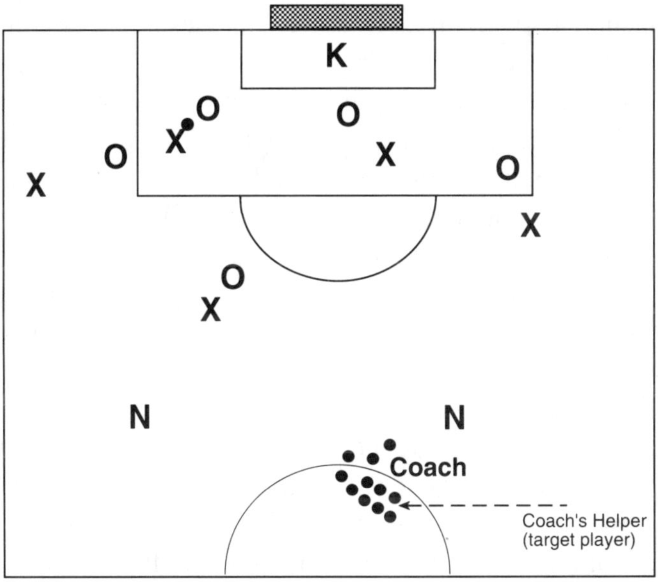

Diagram #44: This is similar to half court basketball. To save time, the coach can serve in another ball whenever the keeper stops a shot or the ball goes over the goal line. The keeper can distribute to a coach's helper who feeds the ball into a location next to the coach.

Shots on goal are one point, goals count two points, and any goal employing the day's topic (wall pass, for example) counts three points. The defense gets one point every time they win the ball, and two points every time they deliver it to the coach's helper.

Discussion, Variations, Coaching Points

The neutral players convert this activity into a 6 v 4. The number of wrinkles is unlimited. Here are some ideas for starters. **Before a shot the attacking team must:**

1. change point of attack;
2. perform lay off, wall pass, or takeover;
3. involve a third man-on;
4. get the ball to the goal line;
5. hit a target player;
6. pass the ball at least 5 times;
7. not pass the ball more than 5 times;
8. play the ball in the air.

If the defense is good, the coach can challenge them with restrictions of their own, such as stringing at least three passes together whenever they win the ball. The keeper can be removed to further challenge the defenders, or to encourage many shots by the attackers.

Naturally, the restriction is relaxed after 15-20 minutes, and the scoring should be adjusted to give both attack and defense equal chance of winning. This match-condition game leads easily into an unrestricted shortsided game by adding one more full size goal.

A major weakness among young players is failure to shoot. Throughout this activity, the coach should encourage shooting at every decent opportunity. Players should be taught to recognize and exploit the half chances. From a distance, players should be taught to look for the power shot and the chip. The keeper can be instructed to come far off the line to present the opportunity for the chip.

Players must check to the ball to get things started. If defenders cheat, simply serve from farther back and send balls over the defense. Chips, high balls, especially to the corners, will force the defense into a legitimate posture.

Coaching Point

Attempt to assess how many ball touches your players will have from the complete session. If you find the number below 800, consider how you could increase the number of ball touches.

Part II

Basic Questions & Concepts of Coaching

25 · How to Run Tryouts & Choose the Team

In highly competitive programs, no team can afford to be without the top eighteen available players. Except for perhaps the professional levels, the best team is **always** the best players. When there are tryouts, the pressure should be on the coach, not the players; throughout the tryouts, the players should feel that they themselves are in control of the coach's decision. While some will make the team, even those who are cut should benefit from instruction as to how they could improve or make the team in the future. In any case, the shortsided game provides the method!

Unlike isolated drills, shortsided play allows the coaches to easily see the whole player in a match condition. Technically, you can see dribbling, passing, and receiving many times and at close distance. Furthermore, you see not only the technique, but the skill used in a game environment. Tactically, you can see the choice of technique and decision-making (when and where to dribble, pass, shoot, and support).

The link between the tactical and psychological components of the game is communication. In the shortsided game, the coach can assess whether player communication is positive or negative. Positive communication includes voice, hand signals, runs, and eye contact. Negative communication includes calling for the ball when behind a defender or when the first attacker has a better shot at goal. Noise is not communication.

The psychological behavior of quitting or staying with it is very clear in 4 v 4 and 6 v 6. Since this is positionless soccer, all players have the chance to attack and defend. Finally, fitness will be easiest of all to assess: does the player lack endurance, or run until spent and then do very little. It is just as important to know when to run as when not to run!

The head coach and assistant should devote virtually all of their time to seeing every player adequately in 4 v 4 for at least twenty minutes. If there are over thirty candidates, this requires a great deal of time, organization, and work. For example, seeing 48 players (6 segments of 8 players) would take at least two hours. But after two sessions, there might be 10-12 definites making the team and another 10-12 definite cuts. Now concentrate on the middle 24 candidates and get that down to 12. Then watch those 12 in 4 v 4 and 6 v 6, switching teams around. Finally, 1 v 1 or 2 v 2 can demonstrate who really belongs. All coaches should compare notes on players.

At higher levels there should be a keeper coach who works with keepers in skills, especially crosses, breakaways, and special situations. The 6 v 6 can use keepers and full size goals. A suggested three session tryout follows.

Session I

Introduction/Warm-up 15 minutes

Group I	4 v 4	15 minutes
Group II	4 v 4	15 minutes
Group III	4 v 4	15 minutes
Group IV	4 v 4	15 minutes

Administration 10-15 minutes.

If necessary bring another group at a later time

Session II

Group I	6 v 6	15 minutes
Group II	6 v 6	15 minutes
Group III	6 v 6	15 minutes
Group IV	6 v 6	15 minutes

See people in 6 v 6 who you believe are definite cuts

11 v 11 30 minutes

Session III

6 v 6	15 minutes for those who will definitely make the team
6 v 6	15 minutes for those who will definitely be cut
6 v 6	30 minutes for those in-between
11 v 11	60 minutes for final cut to 18 or so players

Again, this is simply a suggestion. There are numerous acceptable formats for tryouts, but shortsided play must always be a key element in player assessment.

26 · How to Evaluate Players for Position

Player position is much more a matter of psychological rather than physical attributes. Placing players by physical attributes depends mostly on the coach's prejudice and provides no answers for positioning players with physical weaknesses. But mental qualities are what allow that striker to still want the ball late in the game after missing several previous chances.

The easiest and best way to choose players for team success and maximum player satisfaction is by simply putting them in a 4 v 4 game with no restrictions. Carefully observe them without saying a word; they will show their most revealing and important assets. Some will hang back and support the ball, defend, rapidly change to defensive posture as needed, and/or maybe cover areas intelligently or mark well. Others will probably hang out up front, regularly calling for the ball, taking defenders on, and scoring. Still others will act as links, drawn to the center of action, assisting, defending, and supporting. This always happens! Players gravitate to their positions!

Every team needs a schemer, that player who always seems to be in the middle of everything, who handles the ball more than anyone else, and can dictate the pace of the game. To find that player, try a 5 v 2 +1, with five players on the outside of a circle, trying to get the ball to their one teammate in the middle, while two defenders attempt to win the ball.

Once these mental attributes are known, secondary factors can be used to balance the line-up. This is where such things as speed and skills enter the picture. Of course, the team arrangement is also adjusted to the team make-up for example, can your three midfielders handle the job, or does this particular team require four?

With a youth team, the coach should move people around to teach them various roles. But this should be done over the course of a season or more, with instruction and practice. Making these moves in a game without such preparation usually results in chaos rather than development.

27 · How to Design Training for Specific Ages

In prescribing what developing players should learn at certain ages, absolutes are dangerous. Generally, what's right depends upon age and need. Coaches should know both the age and stage of development for specific players before advising on how to proceed.

The following chart suggests areas of concentration for players 5 - 9 and 14 - 19. The middle area of ages 10 - 13 would probably include elements of both charts.

Age 5 - 9	**Age 14 - 19**
1. Need much technical repetition	1. Too much technical repetition can be boring; need decision-making activities; technique is incidental to tactical focus.
2. Need a great deal of dribbling	2. Need more passing/receiving and team tactics.
3. Little or no functional training.	3. Need functional training basically positional play.
4. Not ready for team tactics. Require much individual tactics learned in 1 v 1, 2 v 2, 3 v 3, 3 v 2, etc.	4. Need team tactics and game plan.
5. Do not need fitness training without the ball.	5. Need interval training, may need fitness training without the ball if they "cheat" in workouts.
6. Need smallsided teams, not 11 a side.	6. Need some 11 a side, but 8 v 8 and 6 v 4 will often suffice.
7. Training lasts 60-75 minutes, with water breaks.	7. Training lasts 90-120 minutes with water breaks.
8. Use #3 or #4 ball.	8. Use #5 ball.
9. Games are 50-75 minutes, with substitution.	9. Games are 90 minutes, with limited substitution.
10. Need small field.	10. Need full field.
11. Spectators are not necessary, and can be a detriment if not behaving.	11. Spectators needed to offer pressure.
12. One official and non-neutral linesmen are okay.	12. One official and two official linesman are best.
13. Need many developmental activities, rather than diagnostic	13. Need diagnostic/prescriptive activities.

28 · How to Recognize & Design Quality Exercise

	Quality Exercises	Poor Exercises
1.	Can be taught in minutes,with demonstration	Require significant instruction and time; needs much talk.
2.	Game oriented, ending by going to goal.	Not a game, but a rote drill, not involving goals.
3.	Competitive, keeping score.	Non-competitive, no scoring.
4.	Rule variations to promote a given tactic.	Standard rules.
5.	Circular and/or continuous motion.	Line drill with people waiting for a minute or more.
6.	Rigorous, building fitness.	Sedentary, involving standing, no body contact.
7.	Up to one ball per player.	One ball shared by whole team.
8.	Challenging, with fair chance of success	Too easy or too hard; no challenge or no chance of success.
9.	Challenge level is raised as success is achieved.	Remains at a single level.
10.	Builds on the familiar, adds a new twist.	Everything is new, or nothing is new; no continuity.
11.	Requires communication (runs, eye contact, etc.)	Requires little or no communication other than voice.
12.	Requires recognition of visual clues, decisions.	Requires only a technical skill.
13.	Relates to matches (ages 12 and up).	Does not relate to matches.
14.	Allows possession by extra players or space.	Prevents possession because of even numbers or inappropriate space.
15.	Provides natural interval training, with healthy work/rest ratio.	Work/rest ratio is unbalanced, so players get exhausted or slough off, do not learn how to pace themselves.
16.	Activity is self-sustaining.	Activity requires constant instruction or assistance.
17.	Activity progresses to an unrestricted game.	Activity never progresses beyond instruction. Never becomes player controlled.
18.	Players are having fun as they learn.	Players are bored or overworked.
19.	Players ultimately understand the value of this activity.	Players do not see the use of this activity.
20.	Players are thinking, curious, asking questions.	Players are told too much, too little, or are totally confused.

29 · How to Use Keep Away

The most important element of youth team development is possession. Keep away is vital to possession because it offers many ball touches and competition under match conditions. Furthermore, games of 3 v 1, 4 v 2, 5 v 2 + 1, etc. can be lots of fun, especially with a new wrinkle each time they are used.

An environment that allows for success would include a large (30 yards by 30 yards or more) grid and uneven sides, such as 6 v 3, 5 v 2, 7 v 4. (Even sides or numbers down promotes dribbling, not passing.) With players age 12 or younger, use no more than nine players per grid; with older players, higher numbers are not a problem, and even 8 v 5 can develop off the ball skills.

Emphasize the following ideas: (only 1 or 2 in a given session)

1. When receiving the ball: move to the ball, receive side on if, under pressure, and **turn away from pressure**.

2. When supporting: communicate with voice, runs, hand signals, and eye contact, make sure that there is always at least one player in the central grid area, avoid clusters of players at the edge of the grid, do not hide behind a defender, open up to give good support, combine with teammate using 1-2 when available, using takeover when first attacker's head is down.

3. When maintaining possession: shield when necessary, beat someone only when necessary or a sure thing, look long first, then short (a long pass usually relieves pressure for almost everyone), use the available pass before being closed down, when possible, disguise or fake the pass, turn to see another available teammate, play the ball quickly out from the corners, use inside of the foot for accuracy, bendball away from defenders, play two-touch when ball needs to be controlled, one touch when under pressure or ball is sent perfectly.

Some possible restrictions for keep away include giving direction to the grid, using four goals instead of two, limiting the number of touches, requiring the use of the weaker foot, finding the longest pass, or using a playmaker to connect on every pass.

30 · Why Choose Soccer as a Sport, or What Makes It Fun?

Soccer is a people's game! It is inexpensive, and can be played year round, indoors or out, by any number of players, boys and girls, from young children to senior citizens. Size and strength does not influence the enjoyment of the game. Soccer promotes fitness, both aerobic and anaerobic, as well as agility and development of the entire body.

Soccer is a player's game! Everyone handles the ball, everyone attacks, everyone defends. Everyone makes decisions; everyone takes responsibility. Yet it is a high chance/low focus sport, where players have many chances to succeed and to redeem mistakes. There is little time to brood over mishaps due to the continuous play. Adult intervention is minimized, since coaching from the sidelines is not permitted.

Soccer is a thinking game! Every player is in charge when he or she has the ball. Players are not asked to just execute, but instead are required to formulate their own ideas in relation to the game plan. Soccer develops thinking skills such as cognition and decision-making that can apply to all areas of life through adulthood.

Soccer is a team game! Each player must work with every team member on a continual basis, communicating with words, hand signals, eye contact, body position, and movement.

Soccer is a world game! As the most popular sport in the world, soccer is played and observed in virtually every land. The game is a gateway to any culture on earth. More people watch the World Cup Soccer Final than the Super Bowl, World Series, and NBA Finals combined! The game is a great bridge to education in terms of geography, culture, and language. Tournaments become ambassadors of goodwill and understanding.

Soccer is a game of spirit more than rules! The rules are few and fairly simple, but always subject to the spirit of the game. The spirit of soccer, like the game itself, is refreshing, valuable, and much needed in our society.

Soccer has carry over to success fulfilling lives because it helps thinking and dealing with the highs and lows of emotion!

31 · How to Maintain Safety Around the Goal

The size, weight, and structure of goals present a potential danger. Promoting goal safety must be a major concern of any soccer program. Homemade goals can be particularly dangerous, since they account for more than 90% of the injuries resulting from falling goalposts.

Manufactured goals, as a general rule, are either permanent or portable. Most newer goals have safety labels. These instructions should be shared with coaches, players, and parents. Whether a goal is permanent or portable, insist on these rules: no climbing on the goal, even when attaching nets; no hanging from the crossbar, even when making a save; and no hanging from the nets, at any time.

Also, in training sessions or matches, allow no other players or coaches to be near the post. Though it is common for people to lean against the post, it is a dangerous practice. Not only can it distract the keeper or block the view of the post, it is especially dangerous for the person leaning on the post. The natural reflex to avoid a driven ball can cause a person to strike his or her head against the post. Coaches must be absolutely certain to keep this area clear at all times.

Diagram #45:
Leaning on the goal post can be dangerous!

Before each practice session or game, inspect the goals. Check that all bolts, screws and connections are intact and securely tightened. Examine all parts for sharp edges, fractures, or protrusions. Determine that the goals are securely anchored. If the inspection locates a problem, take the goals out of service until the problem is corrected.

Also, inspect the ground in and around the goal. Remove any hazards and fill any holes. Check to see that all the pegs are safely in place. Keep count of the number of pegs.

Portable goals are important to field maintenance and safety, since they can be moved to safe turf. But moving them requires strict instruction, since over 60% of all soccer fatalities result from improper goal movement. For unfamiliar goals, a test lift of approximately six inches is a good idea. Before any movement of the goal, keep the area in front of the goal clear of people and equipment! Young players should not be allowed to move full-size goals, and even high school players need proper instruction and careful supervision. Because the crossbar carries much of the weight, goals are likely to topple forward with deadly force when improperly carried.

In most cases, the crossbar must be eased to the ground with at least one full-grown person at each upright working in unison, supporting the weight as the crossbar is lowered forward to the ground. The goals should never be allowed to fall to the ground. A very heavy goal (some weigh 800 pounds!) is usually old and weak in structure; it may be rusting from the inside. It is unsafe to move and should be replaced with a quality portable goal.

With the lightest aluminum goals, several adults can manage over a short distance once the goal face is on the ground and they have found the center of balance. However, the movement of some goals requires six adults or more, with equal support at each corner. The goal should be carried with the face parallel to the ground, each carrier using two hands under the bar. Do not carry the goal by the net rail if there is one; one mis-step can break several fingers.

At the end of the season, dismantle and store goals in an enclosed area away from public access. Otherwise, secure the goals to a fence or wall, face down, exposing no sharp edges. Any storage procedure should prevent climbing on the goals.

Some people have proposed padding the goals as a safety measure.

This makes sense in football, but not in soccer. Instead of bouncing away from the goal, the ball would remain near the post, where several players would converge at speed.

While the aspects of goal safety are relatively few and simple, they are extremely important to the well-being of your players, fans, and coaches. Let your club know that you are serious about goal safety; and instill an awareness of safety issues over the course of the season. Safety is an integral part of coaching.

32 · How Tony Dicicco, Joe Machnik, Jeff Tipping & Greg Deutsch Train Goalkeepers for Excellence and Safety

The experts agree: proper goalkeeper training raises both the level and safety of any team's performance. But keeper safety is not simply a matter of technique, as some have argued. It equally involves the other components of the game: tactics, fitness, and psychology. Therefore, it is absolutely essential that goalkeepers receive a great deal of training and practice in the goal area under match conditions. This helps build the confidence and safety that all keepers need.

For discussion purposes, goalkeeper safety can best be examined in terms of these key areas: equipment, the goal, the ball, diving, contact with other players, psychology and communication.

Goalkeeper equipment is important for safety and performance. Generally, gloves should be worn for all practice with the ball, and for diving instruction without the ball, in order to protect the fingers. One of the few times gloves need not be worn is in diagnosing correct catching technique. The keeper shirt with padded elbows is a help for the outdoor game; separate elbow pads are often preferred indoors. Knee pads are generally reserved for indoors. Padded shorts or pants have become standard, though some keepers prefer sliding pants under non-padded shorts. Footwear is determined by the condition of the goalmouth surface. Wet, damaged areas call for screw-ins; hard, dry ground may require molded cleats or turf shoes. Shin guards should be sturdy and replaced when worn or damaged. Proper fit is imperative.

Helmets may not improve safety. Hard shell helmets are prohibited; they could hurt other players. Soft shell helmets are permitted, but protect basically only against abrasions, and may in fact encourage rougher play. Thus, a reduction of abrasions could be offset by an increase in more serious injuries.

While general goal safety has been outlined in the previous chapter, goalkeepers require special training to avoid colliding with the goalposts.

Keepers who seldom train near the post or with the team are in danger during game time. Training the keeper in a well-marked penalty and goal area, with the team and under game conditions will help him or her remain constantly aware of where the posts and players are. Good positioning seldom puts the keeper in danger of hitting the post.

A basic exercise for safety and fitness is to shuffle step from outside one post to outside the other post in an arc pattern. This develops footwork and an awareness of the keeper's position.

Train the keeper to move forward on all saves; this is good technique and promotes safety. Before training in goal, keepers should master the basic diving progression, especially the technique of always moving forward. They should also be fully aware of the consequences of collision with the post. When they are ready for diving forward practice in the vicinity of the post, the following exercise can be done in the penalty area. The server simply holds the ball at low to medium heights, and the keeper dives forward to take the ball out of the server's hand. Progress to an actual dive for a loose ball. The "W" catch is still used, but one hand is behind the ball and the other is on top of the ball. The ground acts as a third hand. Then serve from 15 feet, increasing the distance gradually to 15 yards.

The obvious exception to moving forward is defending against chips; this requires backward movement. In this case, develop familiarity with the post in the calm atmosphere of a training session. Instead of backpedaling, move towards the goal line from a side-on position using a crossover step. This allows some sight of the goal and post for safety; it also encourages the use of the proper (higher) arm, thus increasing the keeper's reach.

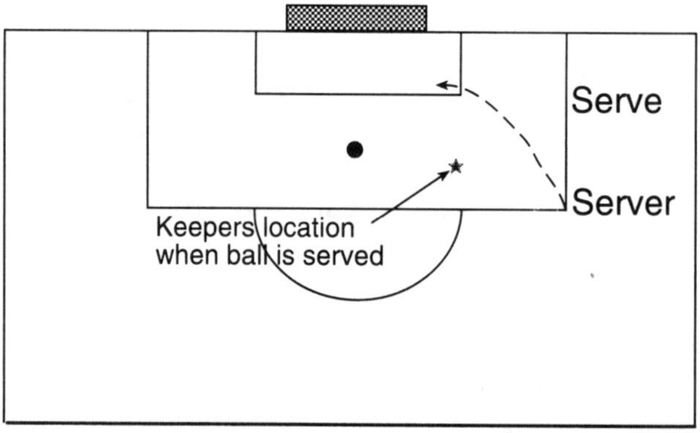

Diagram #46: Train for backward movement and saving before working in the vicinity of the post.

Again, the keeper should master the technique away from goal before working near the post. The coach serves from the 18 yard line. The ball is first served outside the goal area, then gradually served to within five yards of the post.

Training keepers to save chips closer than five yards from the post requires a professional (full-time) coach. In such cases, they should begin with an "inside" path to the post (an arc leading inside the post), then swerve to an "outside" path to make the play away from the post. A crossover step is more efficient for longer distances.

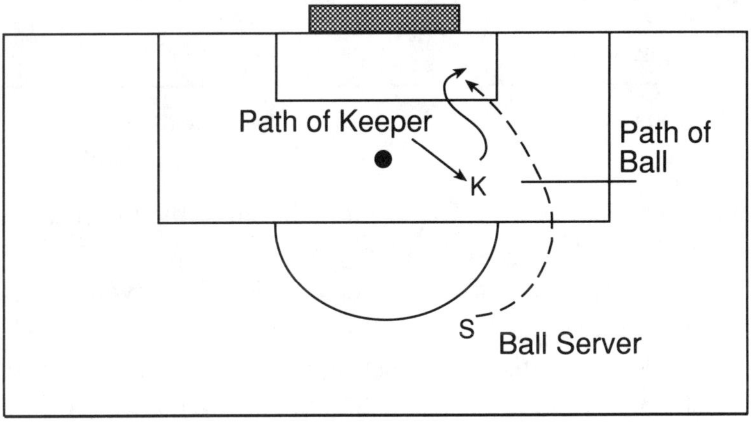

Diagram #47: The indirect route allows diving without colliding with the post.

To increase awareness of the goal with advanced keepers, serve ground, driven, and air balls from both left and right. Increase the pace of served balls from various locations.

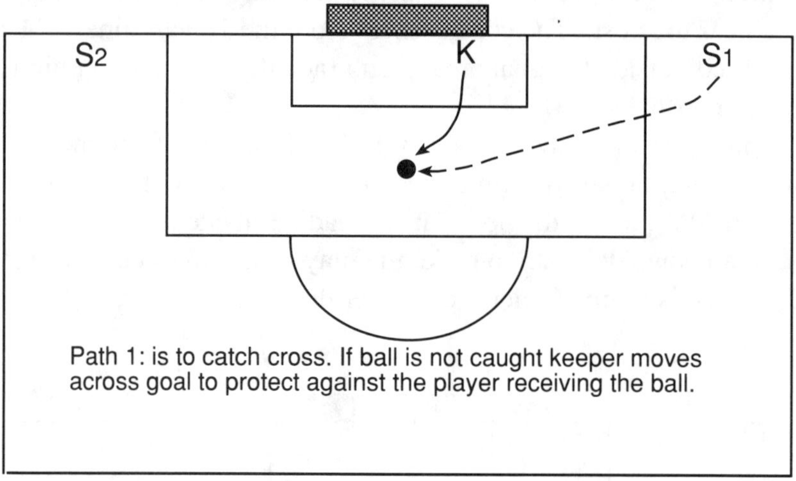

Diagram #48: Serving ground, driven and air balls into the goal area.

Progress to shots from the 18 yard line driven to the far post, and finally shots randomly driven to either post.

The keeper must also be trained to deal with balls served to the cross bar. Good decision-making is vital here. A hard shot may drive the hands into the crossbar; punching or redirecting is usually safer than catching these hard shots. Again, the basic technique of moving forward for the save will help prevent the hands from being pinned against the top rail. Just as important is to develop the mind set and technique of getting the heel of the hand to the ball as much as possible. Finally, keepers should not grab the bar after directing balls over the top.

For the goalkeeper, dealing with shots is not simply a matter of technique, but of technique, tactics, fitness, and psychology combined. The starting block in terms of safety is the get-set position. This is the keeper's expression of technical, tactical, physical, and psychological readiness. The head is up with alert eyes. The knees are bent, with the weight on the balls of the feet. The feet and hands are ready to go toward the ball.

The contour catch (the "W" grip with the wrists cocked forward) is a vital part of safe keeping. Cocking the wrists forward not only cushions the catch, but also prevents wrist sprains. The quality catch is a quiet catch, where flexed fingers assist cushioning. The Kwik Goal Medicine

Diagram #49:
The contour catch; note angle of wrists.

Ball greatly improves strength and confidence for the contour catching skill. Clean, confident catches avoid subsequent collisions.

The next area of keeper safety is diving. Diving should not be started at too early an age, not only because of safety, but because young keepers may use diving instead of the more important good footwork. Diving progressions can easily take five sessions with young players, and must not be forced or overdone. Players often indicate that they want to learn this skill; this is often a helpful guide to their readiness.

The diving progression requires a knowledgeable coach who can teach the technique safely. The lesson usually begins with the keeper in the sitting position, then kneeling, crouching, and finally standing to do the basic collapse dive. No portion of the arm, especially the elbow, should be under the body. The forearms should be out front to protect the face; the upper leg is slightly spread and the knee bent to protect the midsection. Rounding off the body is another safety basic. Whenever possible, use the ball to cushion the landing.

Competence with the basic collapse dive must precede full diving instruction. Full out dives can be practiced in soft wet turf, a sand pit, or on a mat (wear long sleeves and pants on the mat). Work slowly; correct technical errors immediately. But there is no need to comment on every catch unless safety is an issue.

For goalkeepers, diving at the feet of strikers without a great deal of experience and training is dangerous, and should not be encouraged too soon. Anything less than excellent technique, tactics, physical and psychological strength in this case can cause injury.

Yet, at least by high school level, the serious keeper must be trained to deal with the ball at the opponent's feet. First of all, every soccer player, whether field player or keeper, must be trained to jump over or otherwise avoid colliding with the keeper. This is sorely lacking in today's training.

To begin this progression, the keeper is on the ground holding the ball correctly, while the coach kicks the ball easily at first, then gradually increasing force, always working toward the keeper's success. The ball cushions the impact, and the keeper's hands and arms absorb the shock. Once the technique is perfected (the ball stays in the keeper's hands), several balls can be lined up a foot apart. This time the keeper moves along the ground (mainly using feet and legs) from ball to ball as the coach strikes each ball in succession. The coach must be certain that the technique is correct and safe before striking the ball. Otherwise, hold up and correct the technique. Gradually speed up this exercise, always holding back if the keeper exposes him or herself to danger.

Next, the coach can approach with a slow dribble and prepare for a shot while the keeper times the dive and save to stop the ball before, during, or just after the kick, depending on timing and distance. Whenever the keeper cannot reach the ball on the striker's foot, the keeper must "get set" for the shot.

These pressure training and multiple save exercises must be done regularly in training. Many injuries occur when the keeper must deal with a rebound or a failure to control the ball on the first try. Preparedness for multiple saves aids safety.

Forward dives, so-called scoop saves, also require training for safety. Goalkeepers who make this save with a straight spine expose themselves to unnecessary danger. The straight spine collision can cause paralysis or even death. Train the keeper to keep the head up and the spine curved. This is accomplished by bending the knees and getting low for the catch. When collisions are inevitable, avoid straight on contact; instead, create the much safer side on collision.

Diagram #50: Proper technique for keepers is to face the opponent, thus not exposing the back of the neck and spine.

Contrary to what some believe, catastrophic injuries in sports are usually self-inflicted; that is, the hitter, not the person who is hit, often gets hurt more seriously.

Protecting the spine includes not exposing it to body contact. Young or beginning keepers have a tendency to roll or to turn their head away from the charge, which exposes the back of the neck and the spine. Again, the proper technique is the safe technique: face the charge, get the hands to the ball as soon as possible, if on the ground bend the upper leg to protect the abdomen, while the arms protect the face and neck.

In addition, keepers need to be aware of players behind them, as when corner kicks are taken. While it is illegal for field players to charge or strike the keeper from behind, the keeper must learn to defend against the unscrupulous player or accidental foul from the rear. Of course, referees need to protect keepers by punishing fouls against them. And certainly, fouls by goalkeepers should also be treated seriously. In any case, vision and awareness are vital to the goalkeeper.

This brings us to the psychological aspect of goalkeeping. The well-prepared keeper knows the opponent, having studied them at least during the warm-ups, preferably during a previous game and during the early part of the match. The well-prepared keeper has a game plan, and is neither over-confident nor over-excited. The well-prepared keeper knows that passivity or lack of mental preparation can invite needless danger. Safe training is part of the proper preparation for competition. When the coach teaches the proper technique, tactics, conditioning, and mental toughness with the keeper, all with safety in mind, the keeper will be well-prepared.

While aggression is an important element of goalkeeping, some coaches forget that patience is equally important. Sometimes the best tactical decision is to wait, or even change the initial decision. The well-trained keeper uses both aggression and patience at the proper time. The result is better and safer goalkeeping.

The final area of concern is communication. Frequent yelling is not just a distraction; it is a potential safety hazard. Calm, controlled, simple, clear communication promotes safety and good goalkeeping. The basic commands, "Keeper!" and "Away!" are essential to good keeping and safety. But hand signals, body position, body language, and an occasional pat on the back are also a part of the process.

Effective communication between the goalkeeper and the field players takes time. For safety and effectiveness, keepers need to train regularly with the team. This amount of time is a question of age and experience. Astute coaches include the keeper as much as possible in warm-ups, fitness and skill training, shortsided games and communication activities. But they also give their keepers sufficient specialized warm-up and preparation before putting them in goal.

The recent pass-back rule requires that keepers be good soccer players, able to kick accurately with either foot, and head the ball for clearance. Any change in rules regarding the goalkeeper will affect goalkeeper training and safety. While this particular rule is good for the game, it demands more of the goalkeeper, and therefore should become part of keeper training.

The best coaches find ways to turn any rule change into a positive aspect for their team. With the passback rule, the keeper can be trained to initiate the counterattack with an accurate foot pass to a target player. Like field players, goalkeepers need to become total soccer players, and no field player is really complete without some knowledge and experience in goalkeeping.

By now it should be clear that the goalkeeper's safety is very much determined by that keeper's knowledge and skill, which the coach must provide.

A major problem is that many coaches have limited goalkeeper training or experience. Since coaches are legally and morally bound to assure reasonable safety for their goalkeepers and field players, they must make every effort to keep current with methods of goalkeeper training and issues of goalkeeper safety. Camps, clinics, videos, books, magazine articles, and dialog with leading coaches all offer insights into the game from the keeper's perspective. Only the coach who trains goalkeepers for all four dimensions of the game can be satisfied with both the performance and safety of the keeper.

A great deal of the keepers training must be in the goal dealing with the basics of crosses, breakaways and special situations with decision making and techniques given equal attention. Furthermore, nothing will replace playing in goal in shortsided games, scrimmage and actual games.

33 · How Ball Touches Relate to Player Development

Of course, many factors contribute to player development. Athleticism, psychological makeup, a soccer environment, and exposure to high level matches all play a role. While individual coaches and players may have limited influence on these areas, they retain a great deal of influence over another dominant factor in player development: namely, ball touches.

Ball touches are an absolute requirement in every soccer player's development. But this area has hardly been studied or researched enough! Just to provoke some thought, let's take a look at some figures.

It is estimated that developing a top high school player would require approximately 1,000,000 touches prior to age 18! A professional player may need two or three times that!

Is this possible? Can a program offer a million touches over the course of a player's career from age 5 - 18? Here is a sample of what it would take:

Touches From Age 5 - 18

Age	# of Days Per Year	# of Touches Per Session	# of Years	Total Touches
5-6	120	849	2	203,760
7-9	182	784	3	428,064
10-12	274	822	3	657,684
13-15	218	775	3	506,850
16-18	218	735	3	480,690
Total Touches between ages 5 and 18 for High Level Player				**2,277,048**

In the above chart, notice the number of days per year. How many programs offer that many training sessions? How many young players attend 90% of those sessions? In short, few programs offer that much ball contact. Therefore, players need to practice on their own. They will do this only if it is fun for them.

Looking at this from another angle, let's see how many touches per session we can offer our players at various ages. The following chart reveals the average number of touches per practice session for ages 5 -18.

Touches Per Session

AGE		WARM-UP					INSTRUCTIONAL SEGMENT			SHORTSIDED SCRIMMAGE				GRAND TOTAL TOUCH	TOTAL PRACTICE TIME
	DRIB/JUG TOUCHES # PER MINUTE MINIMUM	TOTAL	# OF PLYRS WITH ONE BALL	PASS/REC. TOUCHES EACH PLAYER	MIN	TOTAL TOUCHES	AVG. # TOUCHES PER MIN.	MINS.	TOTAL	# OF PLYRS ASIDE	MINS.	APPROX. TOUCHES PER MIN.	TOTAL TOUCH	MINS.	MINS.
5-6	30 x 10 =	300	2	24	6	144	6	15	90	3	45	7	315	849	70
7-9	30 x 10 =	300	2	24	6	144	6	15	90	4	50	5	250	784	75
10-12	30 x 10 =	300	2	24	8	192	6	25	150	5	45	4	180	822	80
13-15	30 x 10 =	300	3	16	10	160	6	25	150	6	55	3	165	775	90
16-18	30 x 10 =	300	4	12	10	120	6	25	150	6	55	3	165	735	90
				Every 5 sec. 1 pass; 2 touches per player			Approx. 1 touch every 10 seconds			Obviously 1 v 1, 2 v 2 etc. days will have more touches					

Shortsided play will yield approx. this many touches per minute

1 v 1 = 20	3 v 3 = 7	5 v 5 = 4	8 v 8 = 2+
2 v 2 = 10	4 v 4 = 5	6 v 6 = 3	11 v 11 = 2

34 · How to Use 1 v 1 Formats

These games normally use small goals of one, two, or three cones. Adjust the distances and goal size to accommodate your players. If full-size portable goals are available, rotate each group through a 1 v 1 on these goals with keepers. Adjust the grid dimensions on various days; very small (8 yards) fields-encourage moves and tight control; large fields (18 yards) encourage driving and speed dribbling.

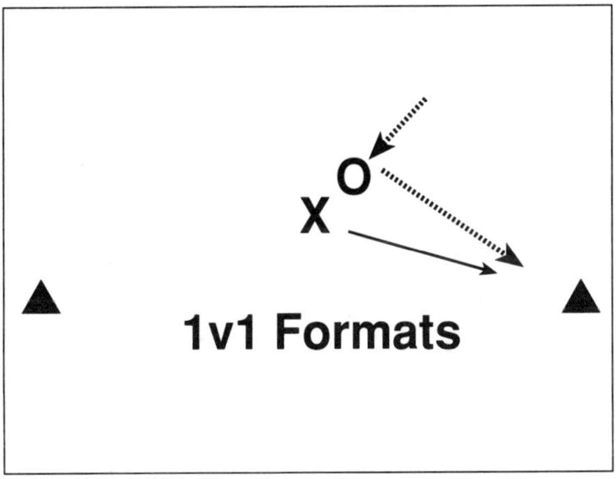

1. Start play anywhere between, but not in line with the goals; either player can score on either goal; difficult to defend, builds confidence in dribbling for young players

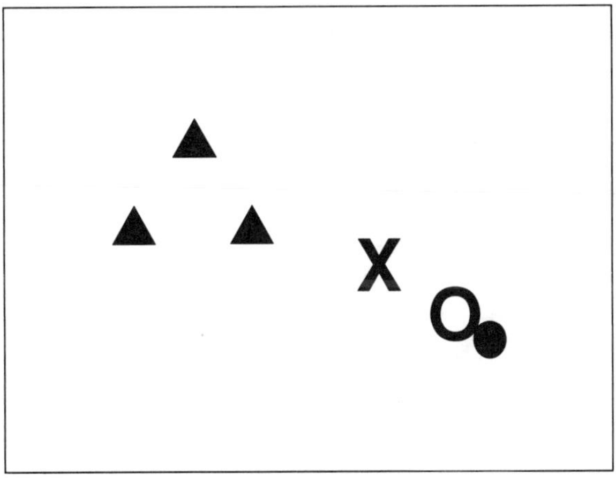

2. Triangle of cone/goals one yard apart; either player can score in any direction; for better players use smaller goals.

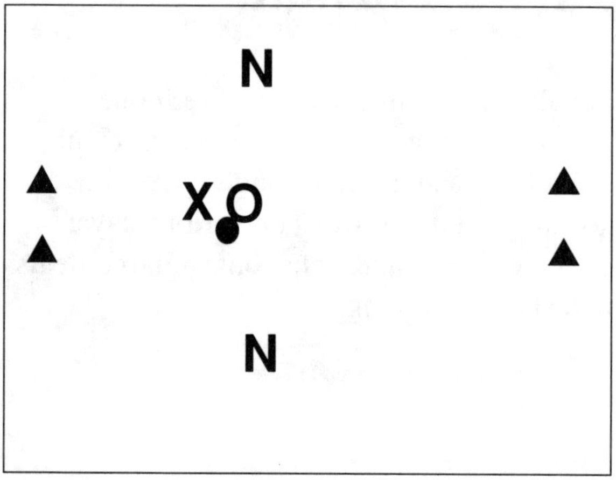

3. 1 v 1 to 1 yard goal; 2 neutrals promote 1-2 combo's; when X scores, O gets the ball.

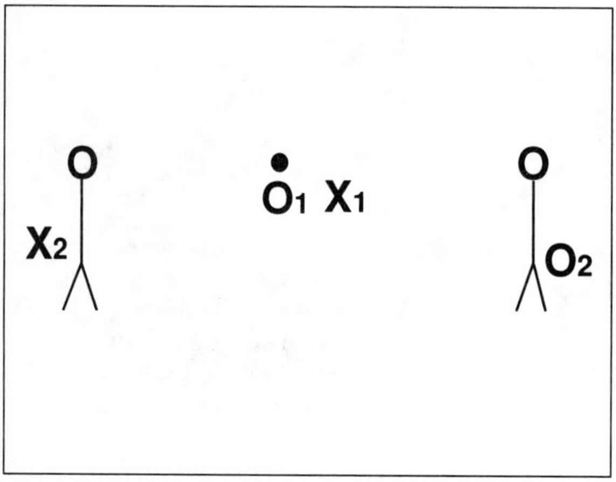

4. 1 v 1 with partners as goals; score on partner's open legs; alternate from player to "goal."

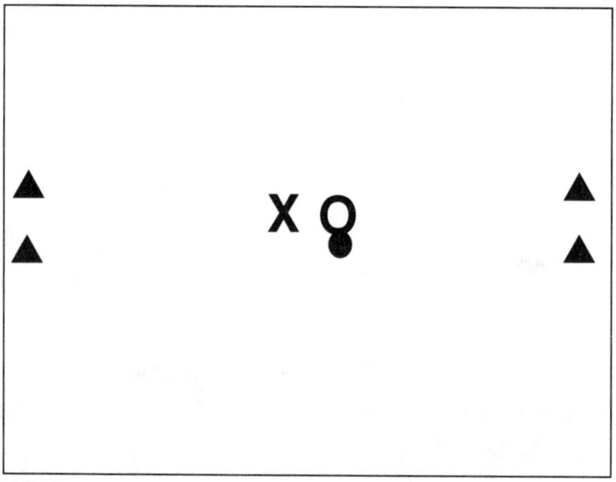

5. 1 v 1 to 1 yard goals; option: one goal only.

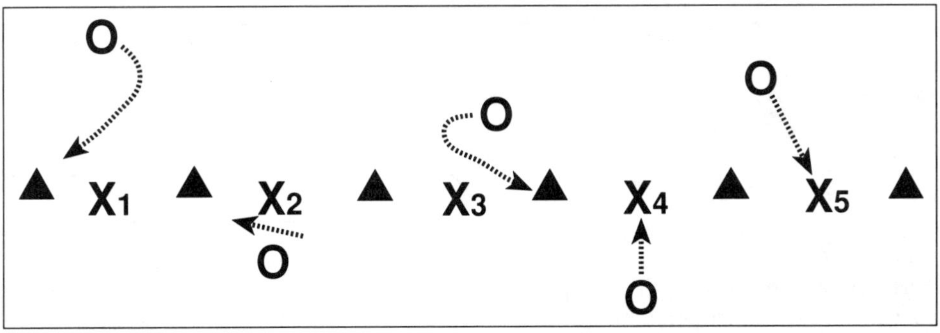

6. Line keeper; this develops feinting while dribbling; keeper becomes attacker when he touches ball. Attacker must control ball within 10 feet of crossing the goal line.

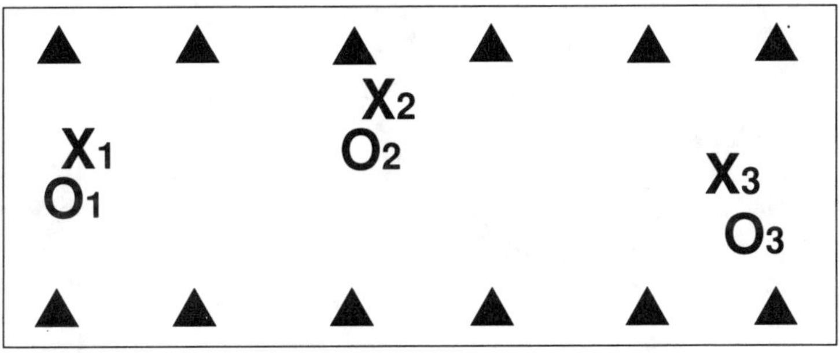

7. Any "O" player can score on any top goal; any "X" can score on any bottom goal; progress to each pair using one set of goals.

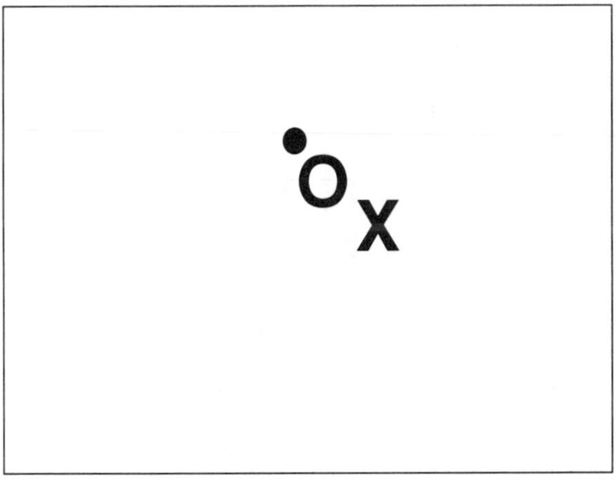

8. 1 v 1 shield keep away; player gets point for holding ball 20 seconds; alternate.

9. 1 v 1 in groups of 3; S serves air ball to O; X defends; S becomes keeper; X gets a point of winning ball; O gets point for shot on goal, 3 points for scored goal. Rotate.

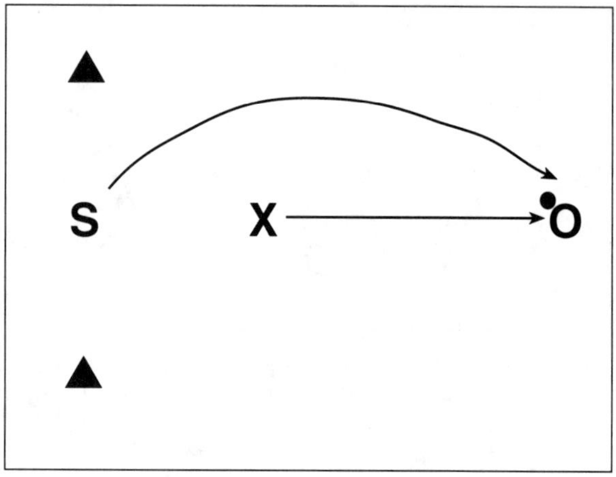

10. 1 v 1 to a line goal; player dribbles over line to score. This promotes many changes of direction.

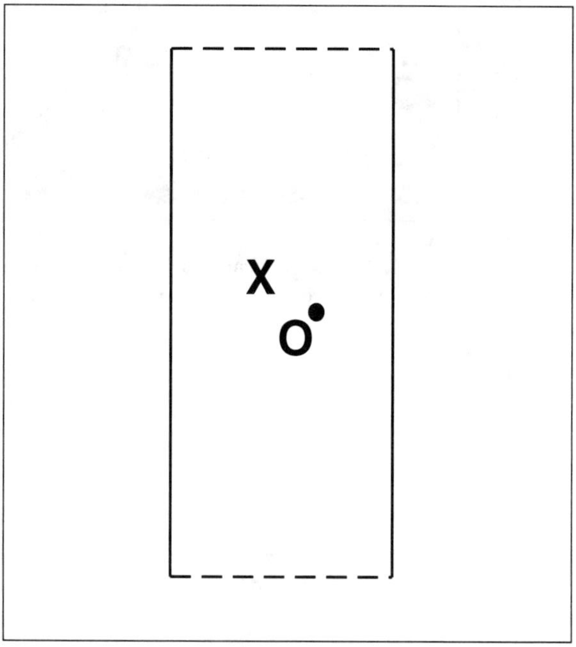

35 · How to Observe a Match

Soccer Game Strategies Reminder

Confer with captains and other coaches before addressing the whole team.

Strategies to consider:

· Are there an adequate number of players behind the ball?
· Is there adequate defensive depth?
· Would the offside trap work better?
· Is tight marking necessary?
· Midfield help needed for marking.
· Zonal coverage would work better because the other team "floods" forward with many players quickly.
· Is the freeback free?
· Are front runners pressuring the opposing sweeper?
· Is there adequate width at the ball location?
· Are chances being taken in the final third?
· Are available shots being taken?
· Is there adequate support of the ball?
· Adequate overlapping?
· Would overloads help our attack?
· Are players too rigid in positions or is there a fluid mobility?
· Is thc ball on thc ground enough?
· If opponent is weak in the air is the air being exploited?
· Is more direct (or indirect) play needed?
· Midfielders are (are not) supporting the strikers!
· Need to attack offside trap (chips, overlaps, direct play, dribble at defenders).
· Need more high (low) pressure.
· Need defensive talk.
· The offense needs more diagonal runs.
· Timing poor, filling slots too early.
· Need more combination play.
· Not exploiting keepers weakness (slow, stays in goal, comes out too far).
· Very physical backs (dribble in box or don't dribble in box depending on officiating or your own team's strengths).

The coach cannot be a cheerleader etc. because he must:

1. OBSERVE what!
2. More importantly he must know WHY (diagnose)
3. Formulate a THEMATIC SOLUTION
4. Be able to explain solution in a SIMPLE manner to his young charges.
5. a) ASK questions of players to check their understanding.
   b) If necessary, clarify solutions to problems.
6. Solicit players ideas, concepts and desires
   (I have learned from 10 year olds when I have listened).
   If no comments are forthcoming immediately coach must be able to bear excruciating silence. If players will offer no comments coach might say, "Charles, what do you think we should do with attack in the second half?" Coach now links Charles comment to another player.
7. Now unify solutions of players to each other, networking.

The order is not a "religion;" some coaches will start with #6 and work back to their own ideas, but the above is helpful. Therefore, the coach must be a careful observer; editing formulating useful ideas for half time talk and have a very vivid picture (recollection) of the game in order to formulate the most urgent and best training sessions possible for the team.

Do not be concerned about minimal input from players on the first occasions of soliciting their ideas. Generally, in the past, adults really did not want their input, never asked for it, did not treat it seriously or the like, therefore, that interpret a request of input as polite, but not really a request for input. I am certain that ALL teams will respond once the players understand their ideas are valued.

Example:

In short, it is obvious the coach must identify WHAT is going well and poorly in the game. Then he must determine WHY? Example: WHAT? Lack of possession. WHY? Not enough players behind the ball and midfielders must be wider. Or it could be, there is no upfront running which is allowing the other team to control our midfield play. Of course, there could be many other reasons for lack of possession.

Another Example:

WHAT? Good possession and build up, but lack of finishing. WHY? Possibly scoring zones are being filled too early, or wing backs and sweeper are never going forward so the other team's defensive responsibilities are very easy to maintain, or possibly the team is merely passing responsibility (in other words, NOT taking available shots). Maybe there is too much aiming and not enough of getting shots ON goal. In any case, LEAVE THE HALFTIME TALK TO ONE OR TWO PROBLEMS AND SIMPLE CLEAR SOLUTIONS WHICH GET AT WHY THINGS ARE HAPPENING.

If you are doing well, what do you do? This is more controversial. Often correction is still in order. Or calmly clarify strengths to complete the match and leave remaining problems for the next training session. Avoid the use of specific player names in the talk to the entire team. Comments about individuals should be made to that particular player after the group discussion is over. The group talk should focus on team tactics.

A moment with each player before the game and at the halftime can be very effective.

IN ANY CASE, WE DO NOT WANT A CONSTANT BARRAGE OF TALK DISTRACTING THE PLAYERS FROM THE GAME. The coach cannot be the player's mind, referee, assistant, cheerleader, and a coach. He must observe the game analytically and make one or two suggestions which are so astute and comprehensive so as to help his team. If the coach is observing carefully, does not allow his voice to interfere with the player's game concentration, he will be acting in a manner of the finest coaches in the world.

36 · Smallsided - - Numbers for a Specific Purpose

Many parent coaches have had many various opinions about 11 aside soccer, but the data of what 1 v 1 or 6 v 4 accomplishes is seldom touched upon. This data is crudely outlined below, but expert soccer coaches know much more than is shown in the chart, and of course, using the **appropriate numbers for the INTENDED purpose of an activity maximizes learning and fun.**

NUMBERS	EMPHASIS OF LEARNING
1 v 0	Develops dribbling and confidence with the ball.
1 v 1	Develops battling, tackling, and shielding, desire and confidence to go to goal; terrific for fitness, body balance, individual defensive skills -- elementary tactics, transition.
2 v 1	Excellent for decision of when to pass or dribble, and how to support teammate, defensive delay and angle; basis of combination play.
2 v 2	Excellent for defensive **SUPPORT**, defensive **COVER**, very fitness oriented,; frequently combination play done in 10 X 20 yard grid with goal line goals; rest periods (coaching points a must).
2 v 3	Very difficult. Often functional for center forwards, movement off ball on offense - highlights player ability to play transition. Used at higher levels. Demands speed of play, decision making, great for possession skills, especially dribbling, simulates 2 strikers against marking backs and sweeper.
3 v 2	Done to help (especially younger) players gain confidence in ball skills, passing, going to goal, teaching overlaps (how to get numbers up to useful locations) - identifying the 2 v 1, combination play especially 3rd man running, and decision making, finding free player.
3 v 3	Fun game, lots of ball contact, frequently done with a "sweeper keeper." Includes offensive penetration, support, mobility and spreading out when the ball is won . . . some use it for match play. Defensive pressure, cover and balance – great for when to go forward and/or back, great for triangle play to full goals. Great for finishing.

NUMBERS	EMPHASIS OF LEARNING
4 v 2	Penetration, keep away, warm-up.
4 v 4	Great for depth and width, two mobility players providing real decisions in terms of penetration; John Rennie of Duke feels this is pivotal and uses it a ton with his college players; skeletal level of group (team), great for training **and league play**, much fitness, allows combinations to take place while maintaining a **defensive cover player**, promotes 3rd man on much more than 3 v 3 - - learn to play 360 degrees; great for teaching principles of play; match reality.
6 v 4 + K	Less ball contact, still very rigorous, allows for excellent width, positions (shape) become more defined and necessary to success. Truly promotes full size goal use, making shooting and creating opportunities for 11 aside match condition. Allows for a regular keeper in a realistic environment. Teaches movement through 1/3 of the field, teaches group functions, is a structuring tool.
6 v 6	Same as above - - Jeff Tipping Director of NSCAA licensing courses uses this a great deal for appropriate movements from one given segment of the field to another. Common at pro level. Combinations necessary to success, fosters 3 man on combinations giving width and depth with balance and shape.
8 v 6	Used by high level teams from high school through professional; can be used with accomplished travel teams for offense of defense. Frequently, big goal for strikers, 2 midfield wide cone goals for defense. Work on offensive balance; team concepts with functional phase play.
11 v 0	For shadow play, style of play, run by a competent coach who does not overly verbalize; it can be **VERY FITNESS** oriented; usually done to habitualize certain combo's in certain areas by specific players, **combinations almost always emphasized**; specific varieties of keeper distribution are often spelled out, should promote use of the whole field. Develops patterns, this is the 'minds eye of the game'.
11 v 8	Many Defensive of Offensive team situations, often done using the **WHOLE** field, excellent for team tactics.
9 v 9	Many Defensive of Offensive team situations, use of the **WHOLE** field. Sometimes for specific types of positioning.
8 v 8	Man Defensive of Offensive team situations, use of the **WHOLE** field. Requires and develops great fitness, good interaction between 'lines', for example, defense and midfield etc.

8 v 10	Numbers down, zone training, pressure the 8, getting people forward and supporting the ball.

Obviously, there are many more useful and functional possibilities. See USSF ad NSCAA high level licensing course manuals, for other details, though this article includes many ideas not included in either manual.

These are the real reasons why shortsided is a necessity. Granted, much of it is not well understood by lay and youth coaches, but at least they know all the experts agree for good reasons, not because of global generalities that say, "Shortsided destroys team". Furthermore, the statement is false. Eleven aside is the equivalent of 20 aside for adults - - more than likely, chaos. Eleven aside of young players who are not capable of using the whole field (changing point of attack to upset a defense) establishes **BAD HABITS** which are difficult to eradicate when they are old enough for 11 aside and a whole field.

Shortsided is reality. It is the way all the greats of the game were developed - - it simulates street soccer. It encourages confidence with ball - - esp. dribbling and shielding. The natural progression from ages 5-11 to the 11 aside game is what has always been prior to the U.S. getting involved in soccer (non-ethnic involvement) at about 1970. The 11 aside at ages 5-11 is recent, new, and most feel has been unsuccessful in developing creative, effective, total soccer players. It is unnatural! It is infact just the opposite of what the lay advocates profess it to be. It is not the real game for this age, but instead it is unreal. Shortsided is great for the youth coach because it allows the ball and the game (environment) to be the teacher.

Suggested match play numbers for various ages follow: Shortsided games present a microcosmic view of 11 v 11, which expose players to pressure, repetition, and most important decision making and FUN.

AGES	GAMES	TRAINING
U5-6	3v3 or 4v4	1v1, 2v2, 1v0, 3v3, 2v1, 4v4, etc.
U7-8	4v4 or 5v5	1v1, 2v2, 3v3, 4v4, 2v1
U9-10	5v5 or 6v6	1v1, 1v2, 2v2, 3v3, 4v4, 5v5
U11-	8v8	1v1, 2v2, 3v3, 4v4, 5v5, 6v6, 8v6
U12	11 aside	

Major focus of training is the underlined numbers. By age 9 designate a keeper.

Chart only represents EMPHASIS; youngsters need all various numbers, from 1 v 1, 1 v 0, through 2 v 1, to 6 v 6 and even 8 v 6 for technical/tactical development.

As you can see, I do not necessarily advocate 3 aside for league play but place very high emphasis on it for training. More than 3 steps is prohibitive for small programs, becomes an administrative nightmare and can be costly. In such cases you could group U5-U7, U8-U11, and then U12 and up.

Defense is hardly covered at all, that is because there is little need for it until the player can control the ball. At ages 5-10 players lose the ball to the opponents all by themselves. In my opinion at least 10 to 1 instructional time is given to offense for ages 5-10.

This certainly does not exhaust the topic, but it at least begins a dialogue to a sensible medial position in regard to shortsided play for PLAYER DEVELOPMENT for young kids. No one starts basketball by going in the backyard and practicing defensive posture and shuffle and playing 5 aside on a full court to a 10 foot basket with fancy uniforms.

No college coach, recruiting a 17 year old player ever asked, "How many trophies does your father have?" Nor has any ever asked, "How many trophies do you have son?" I think 11 aside is advocated by adults because they want to be a REAL coach. Unfortunately, real coaches are highly trained and not necessary for ages 5 - 10. Young players need a very positive person who allows the smallsided game and the ball to be teacher. They need tons of ball contact. They need the fun of touching the ball.

Contributors: *Mike Berticelli, Notre Dame; John Cassaboon, U.C., Santa Barbara; Barry Gorman, Penn State; Glenn Myernick, U.S.F.; Chris Petricelli, Notre Dame; John Rennie, Duke; Sigi Schmid, UCLA; Jeff Tipping, Muhlenberg.*

37 · Shortsided vs 11 Aside

SHORTSIDED	11 ASIDE
*Much increased ball contact	Very few ball touches; detriment to player development; especially technical development.
Forces fitness with the ball · truly soccer related · esp. pacing	Kids can be lazy and hangout easily; **and usually do** inspite of a good coach; with weaker coaches it is virtually useless to fitness.
Forces dribbling **and** passing/receiving to a much greater extent.	Ball often loss before successful dribble **or** pass.
*Forces combination	No need for combinations.
Encourages linking	Often disconnected strikers, midfielders and/or defenders.
Avoids mindless keeper behavior	Forces mindless keeper kicks for safety - - young players not able to build out of the back yet.
Various numbers specifically promote specific technical and **tactical** skills.	Frequently 11 aside matches **DEMAND** much time in 11 aside activity, thwarting all of the other ideas listed.
Develops age appropriate skills. Player at "I" stage develops dribbling.	Player passes even when no passes is on, later age no pass is on and player kicks ball instead of shielding and waiting for an available pass.
3 v 3 penetration, support, mobility 4 v 4 develops simple team shape	Less chance to develop **BASIC FUNCTIONS** Less chance too develop team shape.
*Players become total soccer players, attacking, defending and especially **learning** about the critical behavior of **transition**.	Defenders lay back and have little or no urgency behavior for transition - - do one role instead of all three!

Shortsided	**11 Aside**
Players not cubbie holed for specific role - - (Michael Jordan cut from junior high team) the little player might be a big, patient, strong defender at age 16?	FREQUENTLY, still today players stay in a given role for too many years -- there are exceptions, but even 11 aside advocates know their fellow lay coaches often, if not usually, leave players in positions they play best -- (esp. because of winning mania).
Is FUN! There is action!	Often puts kids in "left field;" right wing-back when playing a weak opponent can go to sleep.
Follows a NATURAL Ontogeny	Is UNNATURAL to historical street soccer.
Allows game and ball to teach	Forces much coaching by the adult. Forces shadow play and other sedentary activities.
Forces attention to technique and individual	Forces attention on team.
Allows offensive emphasis (Generally keeps winning and standings in a lower priority)	Forces defensive instruction prematurely, (let's face it, defense wins and who are the 11 aside advocates!)

This is only a partial listing of the advantage shortsided play.

Interestingly, Soccer America could only find lay coaches to support 11 aside ages 5 - 10 while all the experts advocate shortsided. While there may be one or two experts who do advocate 11 aside, I never met even one in some 100+ opportunities to discuss this topic.

Bibliography

Books

The Athletic Institute; Youth League Soccer Coaching and Playing

Caruso, Andrew; Soccer Coaching Ages 5 -12

Caruso, Andrew; Soccer Coaching Development and Tactics

Coerver, Wiel; Soccer Fundamentals for Players and Coaches

Cassaboon, John and Tom Fleck; Assistant Coach Series U-6, U-8 Aides for Parent/Coach

Cassaboon, John, and Tom Fleck; Assistant Coach Series U-10 Activity Aides for the Parent/Coach

Dewazien, Karl; FUNdamental Soccer Practice

Maher, Alan; Complete Soccer Handbook

McGettigan, James P.; Winning Soccer Drills

Quinn, Ron; The Peak Performance, Soccer Games for Player Development

Simon, Malcolm J. and John Reeves; Soccer Restart Plays

Smith, Small, Smith; Parents' Complete Guide to Youth Sports

Swedish Association, How to Coach Youth Soccer

Thomas, Jerry R., editor; Youth Sports Guide for Coaches and Parents

Waiters, Tony and Bobby Howe; Coaching 6, 7, and 8 Year Olds

Waiters, Tony and Bobby Howe; Coaching 9, 10, and 11 Year Olds

VIDEO

Coerver, Wiel; Soccer Fundamentals

U.S. Soccer Association; Youth Soccer Ages 6-9

Waiters, Tony; The Secret of Teaching 6, 7, and 8 Year Olds

Shattuck, Jape; Individual Tactics Series

van Gaal; Louis; The Dutch Soccer School

KNVB; The Dutch 4v4 Training Method

Ajax; The Ajax Training Method

Hoek, Frans; The Soccer Goalkeeper